THE FAMILY®

MOVIE NIGHTS for kids

25 Fun Flicks to Inspire, Entertain and Teach Your Children

Introduction by John Fornof
Writer for Adventures in Odyssey®

A Focus on the Family book published by
Tyndale House Publishers, Wheaton, Illinois 60189

Library of Congress Cataloging-in-Publication Data
Movie nights for kids : 25 fun flicks to inspire, entertain, and teach your children / introduction by John Fornof.— 1st ed.
       p. cm.
 ISBN 1-58997-214-7
 1. Motion pictures in Christian education. 2. Christian education—Home training.
3. Christian education of children. I. Tyndale House Publishers.
 BV1535.4.M72 2004
 248.8'45—dc22

                                                                      2004009097

Editor: Kathy Davis
Cover Design: Sally Leatherman
Cover Photo: Don Jones Photography
Cover Models: Via Entertainment

MOVIE NIGHTS for kids

25 Fun Flicks to Inspire, Entertain and Teach Your Children

Contents

Introduction

Getting the Most out of Movie Nights

What's wrong with me? What's with the tears? Good grief, it's only a movie. Worse yet, it's a cartoon!

Okay, I've done it now. I've admitted that I teared up while watching *Toy Story 2*. Go ahead and do that little chuckle thing. But what did *you* do when you heard the song of Jessie, the cowgirl doll? The little girl who once loved Jessie has grown up now. She's filled her life with teenage things, and there's no longer a place for the favorite little cowgirl she used to play with. Jessie is dumped into a cardboard box labeled "Yard Sale," her once bright eyes now questioning, as the grown-up girl drives away for good.

My kids were oblivious to my blubbering as I listened to Jessie sing her song. Maybe that's a good thing. But I was impressed by something: the power of movies to move us. When a movie is done right, it's a *moving* picture.

Think about it—why do you enjoy watching movies? I think the enjoyment comes from what we take home with us. Movies at their best give us insight into our own lives. Movies magnify life. The big screen beckons us to leave small thinking, to live life large.

Does your child think like this as he munches on M&Ms, his eyes fixated on the screen? Probably not. That's why you and I as parents read books like *Movie Nights for Kids*. We want our kids to learn to think critically about what they view, while they enjoy a good story with some take-away value.

We also want our kids to experience the fun and fascination of good films, without exposing them to the grunge and grime of moral decay that's so prevalent in today's entertainment. Do you ever feel like I do, though—like Hollywood is out of touch with parents' values and concerns? How else do you explain a movie like *The Cat in the Hat* that's targeted for kids, but filled with sexual innuendo? What were these people thinking?

And yet, when Hollywood does it right we parents line up and buy in the millions. We're looking for movies that reaffirm our values, not ridicule them. We're looking for a tour guide through the land mines. That's what this book is about.

Take a look through the list of movies we've included for you. We can't guarantee moral perfection here. But we can tell you that each movie on this list is an enjoyable family film with a strong moral compass.

And the best part: For each film, we give you fun and thought-provoking ways to connect with your kids and build some memories as you experience the movie together. In each review, you'll find:

Themes: We zero in on the moral heart of the movie.

Cautions: We give you "red flags" about any questionable content. (We also recommend that you preview each movie before showing it to your child.)

Talking Points: Use these questions to spark a meaningful dialogue with your child.

Bible Bookmarks: Discover what God has to say about the movie's themes.

Follow-Up Activities: These are fun ideas to help your kids relate to the moral message of the movie—everything from creating a maze to helping them craft their own "stained glass" windows to taking a field trip to a riding stable.

Some Thoughts About a Family Movie Night

When Jesus wanted to make a point, He told stories. A party-animal son returns home to his dad. An anxious investor buries his client's money. A man rescued from debtors' prison throttles his friend who owes him two bits. These are stories we remember, stories of forgiveness, fear, hypocrisy.

The same is true today. Jesus still talks to us through stories. And if we're listening to Him, we'll gain insight as we watch. *Movie Nights for*

Kids isn't about preaching to your offspring. It's about discovering truths together. *Finding Nemo* is a good example. Kids can witness the dire consequences of disobedience. But we parents can pick up an important truth as well: Being overprotective can suffocate our children's growth.

We encourage you to pray before you watch each of these movies. That may sound strange. But try it. Ask God to teach you and your family His truth. You may start enjoying movies on an entirely new level.

And there's nothing like the closeness of your family cuddled up on the sofa with some pretzels or popcorn, watching a movie together. Now, with *Movie Nights for Kids,* you can also engage with your kids afterward. Learn what's going on inside their heads and hearts. Share with them what *you're* learning. And guide them in a way that inspires them to impact their culture (*in* the world) without being corrupted by it (not *of* the world).

Some Cautions

Take note of our "Cautions" section. To be forewarned is to be fast-forwarded. Generally, you'll find that the TV version of a movie filters out most profanity. But if you rent or buy prerecorded movies, an alternative is a filtering device that automatically blocks most of the bad words. However, while we've tried to select movies that have no profanities and questionable content, sometimes very worthy stories have a few. If your family finds these unacceptable, then skip the movies that have them. We don't encourage anyone to violate his or her family's standards.

Keep in mind your child's maturity and sensitivity level as well. Some kids take certain scenes—such as a parent dying—in stride, while others may be traumatized by the same scene. That's another good reason to preview and pray before you watch—and pray about *whether* you should watch.

Don't Overdo It

We've given you several talking points and activities for most of the movies because we know that your kids will want to watch certain favorites over and over. You don't have to discuss all the talking points in one sitting. You may want to reserve some for another movie night, or strike up a casual conversation later in the week at the dinner table or in the car. Feel free to choose the activities that are most suited to your children's ages, maturity levels, and interests. Above all, a movie night should be fun!

The Heart of *Movie Nights for Kids*

As parents, our white-haired friends tell us that the time we have to raise our children will pass before we know it. All too soon, our kids will be packing their bags and hugging us good-bye as they head off to college and adulthood.

Maybe this is the pang we feel as we watch Jessie the cowgirl sing. We know the wide-eyed wonder of our little girl or boy will one day fade, and all we'll be left with is the memory of how we invested our time with them.

So let's make the most of these days with our kids. Take them to the park and swing on the swings with them, enjoy an ice cream cone together, go on a nature hike and discover God's handiwork. And when it comes to cuddle-time on the couch watching a movie, let's make the most of this time as well. With *Movie Nights for Kids* as a guide, gather the family, grab a snack, pop in the DVD, and let's make some memories together.

—John Fornof, writer for *Adventures in Odyssey* and *Ribbits!*

THE MOVIES

Anne of Green Gables

Rated: G
Themes: Friendship, loyalty, forgiveness, growth, value of family (even nontraditional family), acceptance
Running Time: 3 hours, 15 minutes (can be watched in two parts)
Starring: Megan Follows as Anne Shirley, Colleen Dewhurst as Marilla Cuthbert, Richard Farnsworth as Matthew Cuthbert, Patricia Hamilton as Rachel Lynde, Schuyler Grant as Diana Barry, and Jonathan Crombie as Gilbert Blythe
Directed by: Kevin Sullivan

Cautions

Anne is a normal girl who gets herself into lots of trouble, yet each incident is handled appropriately by her caretakers. In one scene, Diana accidentally gets drunk on some mild wine, thinking it is the cordial that Marilla gave the girls permission to drink.

Story Summary

If you haven't yet met Anne Shirley, then now is the time! Anne is a delightful young orphan who can get herself (and others) into trouble without even trying. She constantly makes mistakes, yet she is lovable, kind, deeply loyal, and great fun. Her prodigious imagination is a source of both laughter and calamity.

7

Part 1

This three-hour story begins with 12-year-old Anne walking through the forest, reading her favorite Tennyson poem, "The Lady of Shalott." Because she is so involved in the story, she is late returning from her errands and is harshly punished by the woman for whom she works.

Anne lives with a family, working as a caretaker for their three sets of twins. When the woman's husband dies, Anne is once again placed in an orphanage. But soon, through a mistake, she is sent to live on Prince Edward Island with an elderly brother and sister, Matthew and Marilla Cuthbert. The Cuthberts decide that, although they wanted a boy to help Matthew with the farm work, they will keep Anne for a probationary period. Anne, with her ability to get into trouble, immediately is involved in several situations that could convince the Cuthberts to ship her off to the horrible Mrs. Blewett (who also has twins), or back to the orphanage. But Anne has a tendency to weasel her way into people's hearts, and she so desperately wants a family of her own that Matthew and Marilla decide to keep her.

Anne is thrust into the pastoral life of Avonlea, finding a world she's never experienced. She is introduced to the sweet, naïve Diana Barry at a picnic and they become instant friends. Diana never seems to do anything wrong, while Anne's quick temper and sharp eye for justice cause her to overreact and get into trouble.

Anne is enrolled in school, where she excels in all subjects but continually butts heads with a boy named Gilbert Blythe who started off on the wrong foot by calling her "Carrots" the first day of school. Gilbert could not have called her anything more galling, for she detests her red hair.

Anne has a fierce desire to succeed in life and studies hard to be at the top of her class. She has to battle a teacher who doesn't see value in anyone except his favorite student, Prissy Andrews, and is plagued by Josie Pye, a snotty girl who looks down on Anne because she's jealous that Gilbert gives the lowly orphan his attention.

Though at first Anne is on probation with Marilla and Matthew, she is soon part of the family. Still, she is falsely accused of stealing, tries to dye her hated red hair black, hurts her ankle when she falls off a roof while showing off, and then hurts her other ankle falling into an abandoned well.

Anne tries to do well as she grows up, and in the final scenes of part 1, she is excited to be serving tea to Diana while Marilla leaves them to act like grown-ups. Marilla tells Anne that she is allowed to serve the prized raspberry cordial to her guest. Anne searches for the bottle, but not really knowing what she's looking for, retrieves the wrong bottle. She serves Diana, then retreats to the kitchen to finish the preparations for tea. Diana downs nearly the entire bottle, becoming more giggly and tipsy with each glass. By the time Anne is ready to serve the food, Diana is so nauseated she only wants to go home. Anne helps her get home, where Diana's mom is horrified to find her daughter drunk and sick. She blames Anne for doing it on purpose. Anne is clueless, not really knowing what's wrong with Diana. Part 1 ends with Mrs. Barry forbidding Anne to ever speak with Diana again.

Part 2

Anne is sad and lonely, watching Diana Barry from a distance. Diana is obviously sad as well. The only bright spot in Anne's life is her new teacher, Miss Stacey. Miss Stacey is an encourager and believes in all the children, giving them educational experiences outside the classroom and preparing them for college and life beyond school. She and Anne develop a special friendship.

One winter night, long after Diana and Anne have been forced to part as friends, Diana races to Green Gables because her younger sister is terribly sick with the croup. Diana's parents have gone to a political rally, leaving her in charge, but she has no idea how to help her sister. Fortunately, Anne has dealt with the croup many times with the twins she used to care for, and she knows exactly what to do. When the doctor finally arrives, the fever has broken, and the little girl is breathing fine again. The doctor commends Anne for saving the child's life.

As a result, Mrs. Barry regrets her earlier decision and not only allows Anne and Diana to be friends again, but also invites Anne to a ball. At first, Marilla won't let her go, angry that Mrs. Barry would accuse Anne of purposely getting Diana drunk. But Matthew steps in and convinces Marilla that the ball would be good for Anne. He also buys Anne her dream dress—one with puffed sleeves.

At the ball, Anne's unforgiving attitude toward Gilbert is evident. For a moment, at Diana's encouragement, she thinks about making up with Gilbert. But then he responds rudely to her, and she returns to her angry cave of unforgiveness.

That night, she and Diana are thrilled that they get to sleep in the guest bedroom. They race to the room and leap onto the bed—surprising and scaring Aunt Josephine half to death. The girls knew Aunt Josephine was coming to visit, but they thought she was not going to be there until the following night. Aunt Josephine is convinced that they scared her on purpose.

The next morning, however, Anne disarmingly apologizes to Aunt Josephine, and they become friends. Anne says later to Diana, "She is a kindred spirit." Aunt Josephine's entrance into Anne's life adds a new dimension to the girl's future. Now Anne has someone else who cares about her, and she has an older woman friend to spend time with and confide in.

Back home, Anne's imagination gets her into trouble again as she plays out her favorite poem, "The Lady of Shalott." The skiff she is floating in sinks, and she has to cling to a bridge until Gilbert Blythe comes along. She's humiliated and angry that he should be the one to rescue her.

Anne grows up quickly, performing an epic poem at the White Sands Hotel, winning the Avery Scholarship, and getting ready to go to college. Matthew and Marilla are very proud of her accomplishments. She is eager to continue her education, but Matthew dies suddenly, leaving Green Gables in a precarious position. Anne decides to forgo college to teach in a neighboring community's school. Gilbert is to teach at the Avonlea school because of his family's situation. Yet, with extreme kindness and sacrifice, Gilbert trades teaching positions with Anne so she can be close to Green Gables and Marilla.

Marilla confesses to Anne that as a young person she'd had an unforgiving attitude toward Gilbert's father and thought she could punish him by not forgiving him. Yet now she realizes that was foolish and wrong, and she tells Anne she wishes she'd forgiven him years before. Anne decides to forgive Gilbert, and the story ends with a hint of potential romance (finally!) between the two.

Before You Watch

Get out an atlas and find Prince Edward Island. Go to the library, or search the Internet to find out more about PEI, its history and customs.

Talk about how things have changed in the last hundred years or so. Have your children call their grandparents and ask them what things have changed since they were young. What did you (parents) have as children that no longer exists? (Wax paper bags for sandwiches! Vinyl records!) Or what new things have been invented since you were a child? Remind your children to watch for things in the movie that are different from today.

Bible Bookmarks

Proverbs 17:17; Ecclesiastes 4:9-10; Luke 6:37; Ephesians 4:32; Matthew 18:21-22

Talking Points, Part 1

1. Would you like a friend like Anne Shirley? Why or why not? What do you like most about her? What don't you like about her? Read Proverbs 17:17. Does this verse describe Anne? How? Does it describe anyone you know?

2. Anne hates the color of her hair. What do you think about her hair? If you could change anything about yourself, what would it be? Why?

3. Marilla says Anne's first prayer sounds like she's writing a business letter to God. Who do you think God is like when you pray? A boss? A policeman? A friend? A parent? A wish catalog to order from?

4. Anne apologized to Rachel Lynde. Did she really mean it? Was she really sorry? What was she sorry for? Is an apology really an apology if you don't mean it? Explain.

5. Read Luke 6:37. Throughout the first half of the story, Anne is judged for being an orphan. People assume she will have bad manners and do bad things just because she doesn't have parents. Is that right according to the verse you just read? What are some of the things people think Anne did that she really didn't do? Have you ever thought someone at school would have bad manners and do bad things just

because they looked a certain way or had a different kind of family than you're used to?

6. Whose fault do you think it is that Diana drank too much of the wine and got sick? Why? Is there ever a situation when something happens that is no one's fault?

Talking Points, Part 2

1. Miss Stacey says to Anne, "The truth will set you free." Do you think this statement is correct? What about lying? Does that get you out of trouble? How can lying do the opposite of setting you free? Find the verse in the Bible where Jesus says, "Then you will know the truth, and the truth will set you free" (John 8:32).

2. "Tomorrow is always fresh, without any mistakes in it." What do you think of that statement? Does it make you excited or scared? Why? Have you ever had a day when you didn't sin or make any mistakes? (Everyone be honest!)

3. Which teacher do you like better? Mr. Phillips or Miss Stacey? Why? Is Mr. Phillips fair to Anne?

4. Anne studies hard to be at the top of her class. In this story, can you see how working and studying hard bring good things to Anne? What are those things? After watching this movie, how do you feel about working hard in school?

5. Anne gets mad at Gilbert Blythe at the very beginning of the story. Do you remember why? Throughout the story Anne refuses to forgive Gilbert and holds a grudge (she stays mad). Do you think Gilbert deserves for her to hold a grudge for so many years over that one little thing? How long do you think someone should hold a grudge? Have you ever held a grudge when someone hurt you? How did that feel to hold the grudge? What does God say we are to do? See Matthew 18:21-22 and 6:14-15. How hard is that?

Follow-Up Activities

No TV Zone

Make a list of things Anne and her friends and family do to entertain themselves since they don't have television. From your list, choose five new things to try, and do one a week for the next five weeks. Then talk about which of those activities were the most fun and which ones you'd like to do again. Make a "suggestion box" so the family can submit ideas for fun things they'd like to do in the future. Once in a while take out a suggestion and do it as a family. Remember, most of Anne's activities don't cost anything, and some involve friends.

Family Reading Time
If you don't already own *Anne of Green Gables* by Lucy Maud Montgomery, check it out of the library and read aloud from the book each night after dinner or at bedtime. Follow Anne through the rest of the books in the series. You'll be glad you did!

—Lissa Halls Johnson

Babe

Rated: G
Themes: Intrinsic value of life, courage, importance of friendship, treating others different from you with respect, the power of love and kindness to change things, the value of individuals who do not have special talents but have love, acceptance, kindness, and innocence
Running Time: 1 hour, 32 minutes
Starring: James Cromwell as Farmer Hoggett, Magda Szubanski as Mrs. Hoggett, and the voice talents of Christine Cavanaugh as Babe, Miriam Margolys as Fly, and Hugo Weaving as Rex
Directed by: Chris Noonan

Cautions

There is some mild language: Babe calls the sheep buttheads; the son-in-law says "for God's sake." A duck is killed off camera for the family Christmas dinner. The fact that the meat we eat was once a living animal is made clear when Babe asks if humans eat pigs. The grandchildren are brats, rudely refusing to eat their Christmas dinner and throwing fits when they don't like the Christmas gifts they receive.

Story Summary

Right away, it's obvious this pig is different from the others. When his mother is taken away, he mourns for her while his sisters and brothers are more interested in food. Babe is swept out of the barn and taken to a small country fair where Farmer Hoggett correctly guesses Babe's weight and wins him. The plan from the beginning is to fatten Babe and eat him. Yet although Farmer Hoggett doesn't know it right away, he senses that Babe is special.

In the farmyard it's immediately clear that the other animals have prejudices against each other based on the type of animal they are. The dogs believe all sheep and pigs are stupid. The sheep believe all dogs are vicious wolves. Everyone believes something about the other animals that keeps everyone segregated in their own little groups, suspicious and unable to get along. And Ferdinand the duck doesn't want to be who he is—he'd rather be a rooster.

Babe is the only animal without prejudice. He believes the best of all creatures. His heart is large, kind, innocent, and loving. Because it is so, he is taken advantage of by the duck, is loved by the sheep, and eventually changes the lives of everyone he comes in contact with—not because he has super talents in one form or another, but simply because he loves others and is kind to them.

Babe is accepted by the animals until he mistakenly follows the devious duck in an attempt to steal an alarm clock. Babe is only trying to help the duck, not realizing he's being used. As a result, Babe is nearly banished from the barnyard family. He's not allowed to "consort" with the duck anymore.

When he first arrived on the farm, Fly, one of the main sheepdogs, took Babe into her litter. When it's time for her puppies to leave home, she is sad until Babe asks, "Fly, may I call you Mom?" From that day, Fly takes the little pig even more to heart and becomes his protector and guide.

One day, Babe wanders from the farm and discovers poachers stealing Farmer Hoggett's sheep. He races back to the farm, sounding an alarm that saves the rest of the sheep. As a result of that and another small incident, Farmer Hoggett begins to take Babe with him out to the fields believing Babe might be able to help him herd the sheep. He discovers he is correct, and Babe does a marvelous job. Babe does not herd the sheep through intimidation but through kindness and speaking gently to them.

Farmer Hoggett continues to train Babe and enters him in a sheep-herding contest—the Grand Nationals. Rex, one of the sheepdogs, is jealous of Babe and attempts to destroy him. The cat tells Babe the only reason he's alive is so the "bosses" can eat him. Babe asks Fly if this is true, and she says that yes, people do eat pigs—even the bosses. Hearing this, Babe runs away. When Farmer Hoggett finds him, the pig is sick. Rex, having a change of heart toward Babe, tells him to pull himself together—the boss needs him. Babe gets well just in time for the Grand Nationals. When the judges find out Farmer Hoggett's sheepdog is really a pig, they try to bar them from competing. Finally, Farmer Hoggett convinces the judges to let them compete because the official rule book does not specifically bar other animals from competition. Out on the field, others laugh at Farmer Hoggett and Babe, but they move forward, ignoring the ridicule of the crowd. Despite what everyone else thinks, they stand true, strong, and courageous.

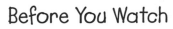

Before You Watch

Discuss where our meat comes from. Talk about what prejudice is.

Bible Bookmarks

Acts 10:34-35; Galatians 5:22; Colossians 3:12; Matthew 22:39; John 15:12

Talking Points

1. What do the animals think about each other? Are they right? Do other kids do, wear, or say something that makes you or others label them as "stupid"? What other labels do kids give each other? Are those labels fair? What does God say about judging others? (See Matthew 7:1; Romans 14:10.)

2. When Fly's puppies leave home, she is very sad. But Babe asks her if he may call her "Mom" and she agrees. From then on, Fly protects and guides Babe. Who protects and guides you? Name some people you want to be like. Why do you want to be like them?

3. After Babe is "warned" that the dogs are really just mean wolves

then experiences the kindness of the dog Fly, he says, "I will never think badly of any creature ever again." But the duck, Ferdinand, is a bad influence, leading Babe to do wrong things. What is the difference between thinking badly of someone (judging them unfairly) and being wise about whom we trust? Should we trust just anyone?

4. What makes Farmer Hoggett different from the other humans in the movie? Than the other animals? (One hint: He sees value in Babe.) How does he treat others (animals and humans) around him? He doesn't say much, does he? But what is it like when he does talk? Do you believe him more or less than his talkative wife?

5. The cat tells Babe all the other animals are laughing at him. That hurts Babe. When Farmer Hoggett and Babe go to the sheepherding contest, all the people laugh and laugh. Farmer Hoggett and Babe continue anyway. What does it take to do what is right even when people are laughing at you? Can you think of a time when people laughed at you? What did you do?

6. How is this story like *Charlotte's Web* (if you've seen that movie)? How is it different? How is Charlotte like Fly? (Both are encouraging and kind.)

Follow-Up Activities

Noah's Ark Diorama

Read the story of Noah and the ark (Genesis 6-8) from a children's Bible or a storybook. If you've done the Train Ride activity from *Sarah, Plain & Tall*, have your kids create a diorama of the Noah's ark story using the box. (If not, follow the instructions to make the box for the diorama.) When illustrating the story, start with the building of the ark, then move to the gathering of the animals, the flood, and finally the resettlement of the earth by Noah's family and the animals. Ask your kids, "Why do you think God included all the animals? Are all of them important to Him? Why?"

Family Password

The sheep have a secret password for other sheep. Dream up your own family password or slogan. But keep it a secret. Our family's was "Banana Soup." If someone told us they were supposed to pick us up from school but they didn't know the password, then we were to run into the office and wait there for one of our parents to arrive.

Create a Story

Write your own short story about an animal who does something other people don't think he can do. Or write a story about a child your age who does something people don't think he can do. You can write one story as a whole family, or have everyone write individual stories and read them out loud. Remember to be as kind as Babe when others read their stories.

—Lissa Halls Johnson

The Black Stallion

Rated: G
Running Time: 1 hour, 57 minutes
Themes: Courage, perseverance, respect for elders, second chances, family ties, hard work, love for God's creatures, honor
Starring: Kelly Reno as Alec Ramsey, Teri Garr as Alec's mother, Clarence Muse as Snoe, Hoyt Axton as Alec's father, Michael Higgins as Jim Neville, Mickey Rooney as Henry Dailey, and Cass Ole as The Black (the horse)
Based on the book by Walter Farley
Directed by: Carroll Ballard

Cautions

Not long after the film opens on board a ship off the coast of North Africa, a fire breaks out in the middle of the night resulting in the ship's sinking. This scene, quite realistically depicted, captures all the chaos—fights for life vests, people crashing into each other, waves exploding over the side and drenching everyone—that would ensue from such an incident. It may be too intense for younger viewers. Also, a scene on the beach where Alec lands features a near-strike by a cobra, ending with The Black (the horse who also survives the shipwreck and saves Alec) trampling the snake.

Story Summary

When Alec Ramsey finds himself on the desert coast of North Africa, the sole human survivor of a shipwreck, his only companion is a wild Arabian horse, The Black. Fiercely independent, The Black at first will have nothing to do with Alec. But after he saves Alec from a deadly cobra bite, a bond slowly begins to develop between the two.

When unidentified sailors land on the island and take Alec away with them, The Black refuses to let him leave without him.

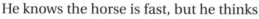

Together they return to Alec's hometown, but The Black is too high-spirited to be comfortable in Alec's small yard. He runs away, with Alec following, to a farm owned by retired horse trainer Henry Dailey. In his prime, Henry was a top trainer, and, although he's given all that up, he recognizes that The Black is born to run. He knows the horse is fast, but he thinks there are too many obstacles to overcome for him ever to be a true racehorse. The main one is that he has no pedigree papers. But Henry agrees to train him and, at the same time, teach Alec to ride. Thus begins a grueling process to turn a wild horse and raw young rider into championship caliber. Eventually, Henry comes to believe The Black may indeed be a very special horse.

Henry decides to take a chance. He calls up an old acquaintance, Jim Neville, the most famous reporter covering the world of horse racing. Neville comes out to the track one stormy night, and The Black shows his stuff during a drenching downpour. The next morning Neville announces to the racing world that a head-to-head race featuring the two fastest horses on the planet will now include a third, The Black. Alec's mom reads the story in the paper about a mystery horse that will be in the race, and Alec mumbles that it's The Black and he's going to ride him. Just then the doorbell rings and Henry shows up.

Alec's mom is very upset when she learns the plan; she's already lost her husband in the shipwreck that Alec escaped, and her son is all she has left. She can't possibly let Alec ride The Black. Then Alec pulls out a little statue of Bucephalus, Alexander the Great's horse, given to him by his dad the night of the shipwreck. His dad told him how Alexander's dad had given him that great and noble steed, and how it had been a turning point in his career. When Alec's mom hears the story, she hears in Alec's voice the love her husband had for their son as well as the love and dear memories Alec has for his dad. Putting aside her fears, she thinks about what this could mean to Alec and she relents.

The day of the race dawns clear and bright. The Black, of course, has never run against other horses. How will he react? Will he run his best? As the horses approach the starting gate, one of them rears, and his hoof comes down on The Black's leg, opening a gash from which blood freely flows. Bleeding, spooked, and untried, The Black gets a horrible start, immediately falling behind by a couple hundred yards—an impossible distance to make up. Or is it? Running like the wind, The Black slowly closes the gap. Rounding the final turn, urged on by Alec, The Black makes a final charge, just nipping the lead horse for the victory.

Before You Watch

Your family might enjoy this movie even more if you have first read together the famous novel by Walter Farley. Your family might also enjoy finding out more about the history of horses, Arabian horses in particular.

Bible Bookmarks

1 John 4:18; 2 Timothy 4:7; Acts 20:24; Hebrews 12:1

Talking Points

1. How does Alec win The Black's trust? What does Alec gain from his relationship with The Black? How does the closeness of their relationship help both horse and boy when the strangers come to the island? Our God is a loving God who gives His children gifts (James 1:17). What good gifts have you received? Have you used them well?

2. Recognizing Henry's greatness as a trainer, Alec puts himself and the horse entirely in his hands and embarks on a rigorous course of training so that he can get the most out of himself and his horse. In the Bible, being a believer is often likened to a race. Read 1 Corinthians 9:24-25. What is the strict training Christians go into? What is the prize at the end of the race?

3. When Alec's mother first hears about the plans to race The Black against the top two horses in the world, she is horrified. What does Alec do

when his mother initially reacts negatively to his riding The Black in the race? What does the Bible say about honoring parents? (See Exodus 20:12.)

4. After Alec's mother gets over the shock of hearing for the first time that Alec plans to ride The Black in a professional horse race, she goes up to her son's room to ask him a few questions. Alec pulls out the little statue of Bucephalus. He tells his mom that when his dad gave it to him, he told him about how Alexander the Great's father first gave him that great horse. Listening closely, his mom hears something in Alec's voice. What is it? How does it help her overcome her fears? (See 1 John 4:18.)

Follow-Up Activities

Family Trip to the Stables

If you live in the city or the suburbs, you may not be near "horse property." However, many towns, and especially those in more rural areas, have stables where horses can be boarded and ridden. Many are open to the public. Some occasionally put on shows. Why not plan a Saturday trip to one of these stables? If you live in the West or vacation out West, there are special places, called dude ranches, where you can spend days or weeks learning about and riding horses.

Horse Show

Horses are trained to do many other activities besides racing. Many horse shows feature dressage, jumping, and other events. Another kind of show is called a rodeo. Events featuring horses include cutting, in which a horse separates a calf from a herd and forces it to go exactly where it's supposed to; riding unbroken horses called broncs; calf roping; and barrel racing. All these events relate to essential activities on cattle ranches, so you can get a feel for what life on a ranch is like by going to a rodeo. Check your newspaper for announcements about rodeos or horse shows in your area, and take the family to one of these fun events.

Just for Fun

The horse has been domesticated for thousands of years. Horses are even mentioned in the Bible (Psalm 20:7, 147:10; Proverbs 26:3). Until about a hundred years ago, horses provided people with their main means of transportation. There are still some people, called the Amish, who live mainly in Pennsylvania, Ohio, and Indiana, who have decided they want to live their lives free of internal combustion engines, such as cars have, and other modern conveniences. If you go to their towns and settlements, you will see them riding in horse-drawn buggies and carriages. Some of the Amish make furniture or engage in other cottage industries and sell their wares in stores near where they live.

—Jan P. Dennis

Charlotte's Web

Rated: G
Themes: Birth and death, love, courage, loyalty, self-worth, friendship, joy, acceptance, self-reliance, self-sacrifice, using your mind to overcome difficulties, showing compassion, sorrow and loss, hope, respect for people with differences
Running Time: 1 hour, 34 minutes
Starring: The voices of Debbie Reynolds as Charlotte, Henry Gibson as Wilbur, Paul Lynde as Templeton, Agnes Moorehead as The Goose, Pamelyn Ferdin as Fern, John Stephenson as Mr. Arable, and Martha Scott as Mrs. Arable
Based on the book by E. B. White
Directed by: Charles A. Nichols and Iwao Takamoto

Cautions
Wilbur is frequently confronted with the hard reality that he's being raised for pork products.

Story Summary
"John Arable wasn't looking forward to what he had to do . . ."
Springtime has arrived at the Arable farm and a litter of pigs has just been born. But Fern has discovered an unbearable reality of farm life, and when she hears about her father's plan to do away with the runt, she races to the aid of the helpless pig and tearfully convinces her father to let her keep it. John agrees and Fern names her pet porker Wilbur.

A little pig can get into all kinds of trouble, and the day soon comes when Fern must give up her best friend to be sold to Uncle Zuckerman down the road. For Fern and Wilbur, it's the saddest day on the farm.

When Wilbur arrives at his new pen, a friendly, stuttering goose teaches him to talk, but not even his newfound loquacity can overcome his loneliness for Fern. Templeton the rat (voiced by the incomparable Paul Lynde) is too greedy and grouchy to be his friend, and the old sheep won't let her lamb play with him because pigs are of a lower status. Besides, it's just a matter of time before Wilbur is made into ham and bacon. Wilbur whines until a sweet voice announces that she will be his friend and that in the morning, Wilbur will get to meet her and learn what "chin up" means. Wilbur goes to sleep, and when he wakes, a gray spider named Charlotte explains many things including what spiders eat and how they are specially made to spin webs. Wilbur is intrigued and excited by his knowledgeable and considerate new friend.

When summer comes, Fern visits and the goose's goslings hatch. The runt is embraced by Wilbur who sings about their commonality "where it really counts." Meanwhile, Charlotte is faithfully planning a way to save Wilbur from becoming a blue plate special. Finally, she has it. All night long she works, and in the morning her masterful skill and selfless devotion is revealed: The words "SOME PIG" have been woven into her web. The "miracle" brings people from across the county to marvel at Wilbur, and as his fame spreads, Charlotte adds new words until Zuckerman is convinced he has himself a prize pig to enter in the county fair that fall. For Charlotte, the fair comes when she is preparing to lay her eggs, but at great personal sacrifice, she agrees to go along with the nervous Wilbur. Waxing existential, she sings about Mother Earth's and Father Time's eternal romance, explaining "how very special are we, for just a moment to be," and offering a rare opportunity in a children's cartoon for reflection on the seasons of life.

At the fair, Charlotte sizes up Wilbur's competition and Templeton scampers off to investigate the goose's claims about the fair's "smorgasbord" of leftovers. Fern drops by, but she is quickly lured away when a freshly matured Henry Fussy invites her to take a turn on the Ferris wheel, and Wilbur is forced to learn a difficult lesson about growing up. In the night, Charlotte creates her last web and lays her eggs. The next morning, Wilbur is escorted by marching band to the grandstand where he is awarded the special prize. Zuckerman announces that as far as he is concerned, Wilbur will live a long life. Wilbur returns to the pen to tell Charlotte the news and she promptly expires. Wilbur is heartbroken, but he returns with her egg sac to the farm.

All winter, Wilbur guards the eggs, and in the spring they hatch and quickly float away. Again, Wilbur believes he's been left friendless, until three tiny voices explain that they are too small to fly away. Wilbur helps the baby spiders choose names and tells them of their amazing mother and what a wonderful and giving friend she was. Through her encouragement, Wilbur has grown from a timid piglet into the pride of the farm.

 ## Before You Watch

Most children will read *Charlotte's Web* in school or for a book report at some point in their elementary career. But if you and your children have never read *Charlotte's Web*, now is the time. What has been called E. B. White's masterpiece is an excellent introduction to many basic concepts like the changing of the seasons, farm life, and appreciation for the variety of God's creatures. The talking animals and fun they have on the farm is a surefire hit with any imaginative kid, and the opportunities for connecting with your child over the many important lessons in the story will be well worth the time investment. Especially relevant to elementary-age kids are the opportunities to discuss the qualities of friendship and the discernment of true wisdom.

 ## Bible Bookmarks

Proverbs 18:24; 1 Corinthians 12:12, 17-18, 26; Ecclesiastes 3:1-11; James 1:5; Proverbs 15:33, 21:30; John 15:12-13; Proverbs 16:3

Talking Points

1. Fern's father wants to get rid of the runt pig. Why do you think this practice exists? (In the book, John says, "A weak-

ling makes trouble.") Do you think that's right? Or do you agree with Fern that killing runts is an "injustice?"

2. Encouraging friends like Charlotte inspire us. What makes Charlotte so good at encouraging Wilbur? What are some qualities of an encourager? Are you good at encouraging people? Read Proverbs 18:24. What do you think this verse means? Read 1 Corinthians 12:26 and discuss the importance of empathy.

3. How would you describe Templeton's personality? Does he contribute to the farm and the animals? How does your personality contribute to the way your family works together?

4. Have you ever been lonely? What advice would you give to Wilbur when he is first sold to Zuckerman's farm and is lonely?

5. Do you know anyone who is very wise like Charlotte? Where does his or her wisdom come from? Where does God say wisdom comes from? Read James 1:5, Proverbs 15:33, and Proverbs 21:30. What do these verses tell you about being wise?

6. Charlotte gives everything she has for Wilbur. Why? Do you think Wilbur is grateful? What makes you think that? Read John 15:12-13. Do you think you would be willing to die for a friend? Why or why not?

7. How does Charlotte feel about her eggs? Charlotte calls her egg sac a "magnum opus." What does that mean? (A masterpiece.) Have you ever created something you were very proud of? How do you think God feels when you use the creative talents He's given you to bring Him glory? Read Proverbs 16:3.

Follow-Up Activities

Weave Words

Draw some spiderwebs on pieces of construction paper, one for each family member. Now have everyone think of some encouraging words to characterize each family member. Share why you chose the word and what that example means to you. Write those words on each person's web, then hang them on the fridge to encourage one another.

County Fair

Have everyone spend some time thinking up something a family member has done that might fall under any of the following categories: "Best

Gift," "Biggest Heart," "Finest Attitude," "Greatest Sacrifice." Write a short story about the event and why you chose it. (Young children can dictate their stories to a parent.) You can enter more than one story and as many categories as you like. When everyone is finished, have everyone read their entries and vote for their favorites. Award ribbons or small prizes (a trophy or toy or special privilege) for the winners in each category and discuss the significance of each story.

Meet Me at the Fair
If you have a county or state fair in your area, why not take the whole family this year? As you wander around the exhibits, ask your kids which skills they would like to learn as a family. (Examples: sewing, quilting, cooking, canning, animal husbandry, horticulture, etc.) If your kids are in 4-H or Scouts, they may be interested in competing next year. Find out more from your 4-H or Scout leader. Though many of these skills may seem "old-fashioned," they can teach important life lessons.

—Mick Silva

Chicken Run

Rated: G
Themes: Cooperation, independence, positive self-image, stewardship, compassion, courage, self-sacrifice, determination, honesty, kindness
Running Time: 1 hour, 25 minutes
Starring: The voices of Julia Sawalha as Ginger, Mel Gibson as Rocky, Miranda Richardson as Mrs. Tweedy, Tony Haygarth as Mr. Tweedy, Jane Horrocks as Babs, Benjamin Whitrow as Fowler, Lynn Ferguson as Mac, Phil Daniels as Fetcher, Timothy Spall as Nick, and Imelda Staunton as Bunty
Directed by: Nick Park and Peter Lord

Cautions

Mrs. Tweedy is as scary as any wicked witch, dominating and putting down her dim-witted husband ("stupid," "idiot," and "lummox"), threatening unproductive hens, and in the film's tense climax, becoming a cackling, axe-wielding mad-woman. A nonproducing hen is axed offscreen and the skeletal remains appear on the Tweedys' dinner table. All the hens are eager to have Rocky bunk with them, but he doesn't accept. Fowler says Americans are "oversexed." Many tense moments occur in the chicken pie machine with Rocky and Ginger narrowly escaping being hacked, squashed, and cooked.

Story Summary

Ginger is one determined chicken. Though no egg-producer has ever escaped from Tweedy's Farm, the little hen is undaunted. And though Mr. Tweedy patrols the wire fence with his twin slobbering bulldogs, she will escape the cramped confines of Tweedy's chicken concentration camp—or die trying. As the hens' every escape attempt winds up botched, the situation turns desperate. The tight-knit group is on the verge of accepting defeat.

Just as Ginger's last hope of freedom seems about to flicker out, an American rooster named Rocky comes flying over the fence, warbling the cry of freedom. Rocky has escaped from the circus, and the hens are ecstatic, fawning over the dashing "Yank," undeterred by complaints from the stodgy old rooster, Fowler. When a truck arrives and the compound is searched for any stowaway circus roosters, Ginger agrees not to turn Rocky in on one condition: He must teach the chickens to fly. Rocky reluctantly agrees, the truth of his inability to fly concealed beneath a bandaged wing.

The flight training gets underway and, sidelined by his "bum" wing, Rocky becomes the obnoxious recipient of special treatment as he half-heartedly leads his gullible crew in a series of endless drills. But soon, a delivery truck arrives and unloads Mrs. Tweedy's newest money-making venture: an enormous pie-making machine. "Chickens go in, pies come out."

While Mr. Tweedy works to put the contraption together, the group dis-covers that Rocky's wing is "healed." His flying demonstration is set for the morning, but unable to face the truth, the phony flier sets out before dawn. He doesn't get far. Pangs of conscience send him back, and it's a good thing because when he returns, he finds that Ginger has been the first sent to be sliced and diced. In a gravy-sloshing, conveyor-belted send-up of Chaplin's *Modern Times*, Rocky helps Ginger narrowly escape and the friends live to cluck another day.

Once reunited, the chickens are in earnest about trying one final plan. Using contraband tools supplied by the compound's own con mice, construction begins on a flying henhouse. Through selflessness and teamwork, the crew of plucky cluckers finish the coop-plane and fly the winged wonder out of the compound, barely clearing the fence.

But the tenacious Mrs. Tweedy has not accepted defeat. In a last-ditch effort to retrieve her unimaginably intelligent hens, she has clung to the string of lights attached to the landing gear. She doggedly pulls her way up and Ginger and Rocky work together to overpower her. As she swipes her axe at Ginger's head, she severs the line and falls, plunging through the barn roof and straight into the narrow mouth of the chicken pie machine. Realizing his wife is wedged, Mr. Tweedy quietly retreats, ignoring her screams for help and the pressure building beneath her. In the climactic explosion, Tweedy's Farm is turned to sloppy rubble, and the gravy-coated Mrs. Tweedy is left sitting in her own failed devising, the excited dogs lapping up all remaining hope.

Life continues for the free-range birds on a protected island in the middle of a lake, and Fowler becomes schoolteacher to Ginger and Rocky's cheeping children, recounting the bravery and perseverance of their proud parents' escape.

Before You Watch

Though the chickens in this movie seem not to mind so much, prison camps aren't fun places. Yet a positive attitude can be a powerful tool for making bad situations better. Explain to your child(ren) that this movie contains a secret about facing difficult situations. Encourage him or her to think about the question "How can you make difficult situations better?" Explain that you'll ask for an answer at the end of the film.

Bible Bookmarks

2 Timothy 1:7; Revelation 2:10; Joshua 2:1-15, 6:25; Psalm 118:8-9, 119:36; Proverbs 11:1; Philippians 2:3-4; Proverbs 18:1

Talking Points

1. Toward the beginning of the film, Ginger tries to motivate the chickens to see past their captivity. "The fences aren't just around the farm; they're up here in your heads." What does she mean by this? Have you ever had a fence in your head about something (fear over a test, a friendship, doubts about your abilities)? What did you do about it? What

does God want you to do about it? Read 2 Timothy 1:7 and Revelation 2:10. How might a bad situation be an opportunity to glorify God? During his time in jail, Paul wrote many letters encouraging Christians. These letters are now books of the Bible. You never know what God can bring about through times of suffering.

2. Rocky's secret leads to pain and disappointment. Are there times when secrets are good? Read the story of Rahab and the spies in Joshua 2:1-15 and 6:25. What makes secrets good or bad? (Your motivation.)

3. Technology (like the chicken pie machine) often makes things easier and saves time or money by eliminating the need to do things by hand. In the United States and other highly developed parts of the world, there is a lot of technology to make our lives easier. But what happens if the technology breaks down or doesn't work properly? Is it wrong to depend on technology too much? Read Psalm 118:8-9. What can happen if you trust something else more than God?

4. Rocky is dishonest about being able to fly. What happens as a result? Have you ever told a lie? What happened? Read Psalm 119:36 and Proverbs 11:1. What do you think would happen if people knew you as a liar? Why is it so important for people to trust us?

5. In this movie, the chickens act more human than the heartless Tweedys. Why do you think Mrs. Tweedy is so mean? Why does she plan to make the chickens into pies? Why do you suppose greed makes people mean? Read about selflessness in Philippians 2:3-4. Who shows this attitude in the movie? (Rocky does when he saves Ginger from the pie machine. Also, Fowler does when he offers to fly the henhouse.)

6. Have you ever thought of what real chickens would say if they could talk? One of the directors of *Chicken Run*, Nick Park, says he got the idea for the movie when he thought of a chicken using a spoon to dig a hole and escape under a fence. Have you ever been inspired to do something by a story or an idea? Where do you think that inspiration came from? Is all artistic inspiration from God? How can you tell?

7. The DVD version of the film includes a behind-the-scenes look at how much effort went into making this movie. A full day's work on this 85-minute film resulted in about two and a half seconds of film. Averaged out, that's a minimum of 2,040 days or just about five and a half years! Have you ever spent a long time building or working toward something? Talk about how you felt when you were finally finished.

8. When you're on a team, using everyone's particular talents is

important. Is there something you do really well that could help your "team" (your family)? How?

Follow-Up Activity
Flying Henhouse

Looking for some egg-citement? Take on this team-building exercise: Build a flying henhouse! The object is to get the henhouse to fly using all your creative talents and whatever you have available. The one rule is, you have to build it as a team. Have the whole team brainstorm what items are available and how best it should be put together. Then randomly choose one person to be in charge of gluing, another cutting, another quality control, etc. Use feathers, construction paper, balloons, plastic soda containers, toothpicks, Popsicle sticks, etc. When you're all done, take it outside and see how far it will "fly." Read Proverbs 18:1. Why is being able to work as a team so important?

Just for Fun

If you've ever tried making hundreds of chickens out of clay, you know how difficult making this movie with clay characters would have been. Fortunately the directors of the film, Nick Park and Peter Lord, had some experience on the "Wallace and Grommit" movies. For *Chicken Run*, they invented "foamation"—a technique that uses pieces of cast foam to make all the different moving parts of the characters. All those chickens were foam, not clay.

—*Mick Silva*

Finding Nemo

Rated: G
Themes: Courage, overcoming fears, acceptance of physical differences, perseverance
Running Time: 1 hour, 30 minutes
Starring: The voices of Albert Brooks as Marlin, Ellen DeGeneres as Dory, Alexander Gould as Nemo, Willem Dafoe as Gill, Geoffrey Rush as Nigel, Andrew Stanton as Crush, and Elizabeth Perkins as Coral
Directed by: Andrew Stanton

Cautions

Beginning with the attack on Nemo's parents and followed by many intense undersea encounters for Marlin and Dory, this movie could be upsetting to younger children. Dory credits evolution for making her a fast swimmer. Seagulls poop on Marlin and Dory. Close-ups of the dentist working on people's mouths provide a couple of unsavory moments. One man screams as the drill sinks into his tooth. A young squid expels a cloud of ink every time she's frightened. The first time it happens, she says, "You guys made me ink." Flatulence is used as the punch line for a joke. Several fish belch loudly.

Story Summary

Marlin and Coral are two young clown fish in love—and they are waiting expectantly for their babies to hatch. Life is good until a ferocious barracuda kills Coral and devours her offspring, leaving behind the frightened Marlin and a single tiny egg. The lone egg, named Nemo, soon hatches, and the baby clown fish grows into a little boy clown fish who's ready for fish school. But Marlin, still wary from his bar-racuda experience, is not very happy about turning Nemo loose in the big blue sea. "It's dangerous out there," he repeatedly tells the lad. To make matters more frightening for Marlin, Nemo has a "disability"—one of his fins is much smaller than the other. Thus it is more difficult for Nemo to swim in a straight line. He is not like other fish, and his father is worried that his disability will put him into peril.

Time has a way of marching forward whether you want it to or not, though, and one day Marlin relents and takes Nemo to school. Life is good until Nemo, caving in to peer pres-sure, disobeys the admonition to stay out of the open sea and is snatched from school by a scuba diver. Soon, Nemo finds himself in a fish tank in a dentist's office in Sydney, Australia. Devastated, Marlin determines to search the seven seas for his boy.

Setting out on his own, Marlin soon meets Dory, a fish with short-term memory prob-lems, which is a running gag through-out the movie. Though she's often a nuisance, Dory is delightful and good-hearted. A steadfast friend, she sticks with Marlin in spite of all the danger. And Dory knows how to read, a skill that comes in handy when Nemo's fishnapper leaves behind his diving mask with his address written on it.

Their journey takes them through a variety of dangers. First they meet two sharks trying to kick the meat habit, so to speak. (One shark's falling off the wagon—temporarily—provides a few intense moments.) Mines left over from the war explode. Marlin also ignores advice from the friendly "locals" and soon finds himself in peril with jellyfish and a scary deep-sea creature. Other creatures are more friendly and helpful. Surfer-dude sea turtles rescue Marlin from a par-alyzing jellyfish sting.

Meanwhile, the fish in the tank fear for Nemo's life because the den-tist intends for Nemo to be a gift for his niece, who tends to be far too rough with fish. The fish band together to help Nemo get back to his dad by devising an elaborate escape plan with the help of a friendly pelican.

The attempt seems to be momentarily successful, but more twists in the plot cause Marlin to mistakenly believe that Nemo is dead, and he gives up the search. But with the help of others, Nemo and his father are finally reunited. In the process, all learn a lesson about teamwork and self-sacrifice—and just how far a parent will go to find his child.

Before You Watch

Discuss the beautiful colors of the fish and the coral reef and what a great artist God is. Also discuss how, in nature, bigger fish eat smaller fish to survive.

Bible Bookmarks

Luke 15:4-6; Colossians 3:20; Ecclesiastes 4:9-12; Deuteronomy 31:6

Talking Points

1. The barracuda lies in wait to attack Marlin and Coral. Why are there such "bad" fish in the ocean? (Read Genesis 3:17-19 and Romans 8:20-22.)

2. Nemo wants to go to school, but his dad won't let him. What should we do in such situations? (Read Colossians 3:20.)

3. Even though he is warned it's dangerous, Marlin is determined to head into the unknown to save Nemo. Why? (Read Luke 15:4-6.)

4. Dory is flighty and sometimes a nuisance to Marlin, but she really wants to help. What should we do with people like that? (Read 1 Samuel 16:7.)

5. Marlin is warned not to swim above a rock formation, but he doesn't listen to the advice and finds himself in great danger. What can we learn from this? (Read Proverbs 27:17.)

6. The fish in the tank know they all need to work together to help Nemo escape. Why is this? (Read Proverbs 17:17, Ecclesiastes 4:9-12, and Galatians 6:2.)

7. Nemo realizes that for the plan to work, he must be willing to sacrifice his life to help the others. (Read John 15:13.)

Follow-Up Activities
A Parent's Love for His Son
A good parent will go to any length to save his or her child. Example from the movie: Marlin's decision to set off into the unknown to find Nemo.

Play hide-and-seek. (You might want to restrict it to the indoors to cut down on the number of possible hiding places.) Make a big deal of searching all over the house or yard, even if you know where the child is hiding.

After you find everyone, ask these questions: Did you think I would give up looking for you? (No. A loving parent will never give up on his children.) Does God keep looking even if we don't want to be found? (Yes.)

Read Deuteronomy 31:6. Discuss why we should have courage that God will help us through dangerous times.

Finding Fish
Get a book about fish or the oceans, or find a Web site that features fish, and help your kids learn to identify at least 10 colorful fish from the pictures. Ask your kids if they know what day God created the fish. Read about the creation of the seas in Genesis 1:20-23. Take your kids to a pet store or an aquarium and see how many of the 10 fish they can find and identify. If your family decides to get an aquarium of your own, be sure to find out all you can about the needs of your fish so they will be properly cared for.

Fish Mobile
Find some pictures of colorful fish to use as models. Provide a stack of construction paper, scissors, paints and other art supplies, and a stapler or needle and thread. Have each family member choose a fish to make for your mobile. Stack two pieces of paper together, draw the fish, and cut out both layers of paper. (Parents can help younger children.) Stuff with shredded paper or cotton balls, then staple or sew around the edges. Let everyone paint or color his or her fish. When dry, tie each fish

to a different length of string, tie the strings onto a stick, and hang the mobile from the ceiling. Talk about how God must love color and variety to have made so many different kinds of fish.

 ## Just for Fun

Marlin and Nemo are clown fish. Sales of clown fish skyrocketed around the world after the release of *Finding Nemo*.

—*Tom Neven*

Homeward Bound: The Incredible Journey

Rated: G
Themes: Courage, loyalty, faithfulness, trust, nobility, friendship, perseverance, personal growth, importance of family, sacrifice, faith, home, love
Running Time: 1 hour, 24 minutes
Starring: The voices of Michael J. Fox as Chance, Sally Field as Sassy, and Don Ameche as Shadow. Also starring actors Don Alder as Molly's father, Robert Hays as Bob Seaver, Kim Greist as Laura Seaver, Jean Smart as Kate, Veronica Lauren as Hope, Devin Chevalia as Jamie, and Benj Thall as Peter
Directed by: Duwayne Dunham

Cautions

There is some mild language, mostly "butt" jokes. For example, Sassy calls Chase a flat-faced butt-sniffer.

Story Summary

Three animals, Shadow, an aging golden retriever; Chance, a young mongrel not much more than a pup; and Sassy, a fastidious Himalayan cat, make an incredible journey over the Sierra Nevada Mountains in Northern California to get back to their home. The animals are left at the ranch of a friend of their owners' family when the stepdad takes an interim position at the University of California at Berkeley. When the owner of the ranch moves the herd to high pasture, the animals think they have been abandoned. Shadow, the leader of the group, decides he's going to head for home, which he believes is just over the hills east of them. The other two agree and they set out.

As they crest the top of the first line of hills, instead of seeing their home below them, they encounter seemingly endless mountains. It's almost dark, and they need to make a decision: go forward or turn back. Shadow encourages them to keep going, so they do. Thus begins a series of wonderful adventures as well as some real bonding among animals that seemingly don't have a lot in common. On the adventure side, Sassy gets swept over a waterfall despite Shadow's and Chance's best efforts to save her. Then the three encounter a mountain lion, and they have to work together to figure out how to evade it. After that, they discover a frightened little girl, separated from her family on a hike. They comfort her, keeping her warm during the night until Shadow hears a rescue party coming next morning and leads them to her.

As the trio nears the home-stretch, they are captured by humane society workers and put in an animal shelter. Chance, who was rescued from the dog pound by his young owner, Jamie, thinks their days are up. What they don't know is that they're simply being detained for a short period until their owners can come to get them. In a wonderfully comic scene, the animals make their escape just as the family pulls up in their car to take them home.

Finally, when they're just a few miles from home, Shadow falls into a deep pit with steep sides. Since it has rained recently, the sides of the pit are slippery. Shadow has also injured himself from the fall. He makes several valiant efforts to climb out, but he just doesn't have the energy to make it. Shadow tells the others to go on without him. Chance slides down into the pit and offers Shadow encouragement, even as Shadow has been encouraging the others throughout their long ordeal. Finally, through an almost super-dog effort, Shadow makes it to the top.

The scene shifts to the family. They've returned home from the shelter, saddened because the animals were gone and seemingly lost forever. As they're in the backyard thinking about their loss, they hear a bark. Chance appears over a rise and runs to them. Then Sassy comes. But where's Shadow? Peter, his owner, thinks he's too old to have made the long and arduous trip over the mountains. As they begin to go back inside, they hear the rustling of the grass. They turn, and it's Shadow, limping home.

Before You Watch

Since Chance originally came from the dog pound, you might want to take your kids to the local animal shelter to see how it works and observe what the conditions are like for the animals. Perhaps you can also have a discussion about how money is provided to take care of the animals. (Warning: Your kids may try to talk you into adopting a pet.) For younger or more sensitive children, though, the stark realities of an animal shelter may be too much for them to handle, so use your judgment on this one.

Bible Bookmark
1 Corinthians 13:13

Talking Points

1. Sometimes families have to make hard choices that seem to have a negative effect on some of the family members. Could anything have been done differently to prevent the animals from escaping? What?

2. When things go wrong in families, we often want to blame someone. What happens when the family discovers that the animals are gone? Who does Peter blame? Does he have a right to be mad at this person? How does Peter's stepfather handle this situation? Have you ever blamed someone for something that really wasn't his or her fault? Has anyone ever blamed you for something you didn't do? How did you feel about that?

3. The animals, who represent a "blended family" as much as their owners, have got to learn some hard lessons if they are going to make it over the mountains. What are some of these lessons? Do you think the movie does a good job of portraying the hardships the animals face? Is it realistic?

4. The trip home for the animals is long and hard. What do the animals discover about themselves as they trek across the mountains? Can you think of some ways the animals' journey home to their family is like our earthly journey toward heaven? (Life on earth can be hard, it can be filled with setbacks and disappointments, etc.)

5. When Shadow is in the pit, what is it that gives him the courage and energy to climb out?

Follow-Up Activities

Bicker, Bicker

Sassy and Chance bicker a lot, just like kids (and grown-ups) sometimes do. Look up the meaning of the word *bicker* in the dictionary. Does anyone in your house bicker? See how many days (or hours) the bickerers can go without quarreling. Hang a piece of paper on the fridge. When a fight starts up, write down the day and time of the argument, along with the names of the perpetrators and what the fight's about.

At the end of one week, add up the incidents and discuss them. Do some family members bicker more than others? What do they fight about? Brainstorm ways to bicker less, and list those ideas on a clean sheet of paper. Write this verse at the top: "He who loves a quarrel loves sin" (Proverbs 17:19a). Hang the paper in a prominent place to remind everyone of the new "rules" about getting along.

Cooperation

The animals had to work together to get home. We call this *cooperating*. Your family can learn to work together by putting together a kit. Purchase a model car, airplane, dollhouse, or other kit. (Make sure it's appropriate for the ages of your children—the simpler the better for younger kids.) Assign certain tasks to each family member.

After the kit is assembled, serve a snack and talk about what it was like to work together. Did anyone want to do someone else's job? Did anyone express unhappiness over which job he or she got to do? Did anyone try to boss others around and tell them what to do? When did the family cooperate? Was that more fun than not cooperating? Talk about ways you work together as a family.

—*Jan P. Dennis*

Ice Age

Rated: PG
Themes: Courage, loyalty, importance of family, forgiveness, acceptance of others despite annoying habits
Running Time: 1 hour, 20 minutes
Starring: The voices of Ray Romano as Manny, John Leguizamo as Sid, Denis Leary as Diego, Goran Visnjic as Soto, and Jack Black as Zeke
Directed by: Chris Wedge

Cautions

Some children might be scared by the prospect of a baby being eaten by vicious saber-toothed tigers, as well as a death scene. There is some mild Looney Tunes–style violence as well as mild "poop" humor. Beware of subtle references to evolution, too. Sid hot-tubs with a pair of female sloths and acts as if he's looking for a mate. Two rhinoceros characters appear to be gay.

Story Summary

With winter's fury bearing down, a colorful convoy of pre-historic animals begins migrating south. A woolly mammoth named Manny heads in the opposite direction and is soon joined by a sloth named Sid, a lazy, jabbering social outcast with a knack for finding trouble.

At the same time, a human tribe prepares to break camp, but before they get the chance, they're attacked by saber-toothed tigers. The pack is led by the vengeful Soto, bent on snatching a baby to avenge the killing of half his pack. The men grab spears and try to fight off the beasts, but they can't stop one cat named Diego from cornering a mother and child atop a raging waterfall. The desperate woman jumps.

51

Soto orders Diego to retrieve the infant before returning to the group. Mom somehow survives the fall, and before disappearing beneath the frigid water, she hands off her little bundle to Manny and Sid. Manny, a disgruntled loner, wants nothing to do with the tiny human, but Sid thinks they should return the baby to his "herd" (family) and says he'll take care of him. "You can't even take care of yourself," Manny grumbles.

Diego tries to steal the baby, but Manny rescues him and becomes the child's protector. Thwarted in his efforts, Diego changes his tactics. He convinces Manny and Sid that only *his* tracking skills will help them find the humans. While he realizes that Diego's tracking skills are important to their mission, Manny is not fooled by the wily feline and makes him lead the way. At night Manny wraps his trunk around the baby, protecting him from the elements and Diego.

Along the way, the shell Manny has built around himself starts to crack to reveal a genuinely compassionate guy. Sid must deal with his own problems—a pair of prehistoric rhinos he's managed to antagonize—while Diego continues to plot ways to separate the baby from the two.

Two tigers come by night to tell Diego that Soto is waiting for the baby. Diego tells them to tell Soto that he's coming with the baby—*and* a mammoth, something that should raise his esteem in the pack. He tells them to be prepared: They'll need the whole pack to bring the mammoth down. They agree on an ambush point.

The next day, Diego tells Manny and Sid they'll have to take a shortcut if they are going to catch up with the humans. (Naturally, Soto and his pack will be waiting.) But as they near the final pass, Diego falls and Manny rescues him, putting his own life in danger. "Why did you do that? You could have died trying to save me," Diego says. "That's what you do in a herd—you look out for each other," Manny replies. Diego and Sid later muse about this and Sid says, "I've never had a friend who would risk his life for me." The cat agrees, "Yeah, Manny's . . . He's a good guy."

When it comes time to spring the trap and turn the baby over to Soto, Diego is of two minds. Will he betray the team, or will he do the right thing? When the pack corners Manny, he defends Manny and is badly wounded. Sid tries to get Diego to go with them, but he tells them to go on. Sid tells him that he didn't have to fight off the cats. "That's what you do in a herd," Diego replies. Manny, Sid, and the baby leave Diego behind out of necessity: If the humans get through the pass, they'll never catch them.

They meet up with the humans and turn the baby over to the father. Just as they turn to leave, Diego appears over the rise. With that, the trio heads south, leaving the baby with his human herd.

Before You Watch

Kids might better understand the setting of the movie if you first discuss the Ice Age—the prehistoric era, not the movie—with them. Explain that saber-toothed tigers and woolly mammoths are now extinct. Some icy-cold treats such as ice cream, fudge bars, or Popsicles would make good snacks for this movie.

Bible Bookmarks

Proverbs 17:17; John 15:13; Colossians 3:12

Talking Points

1. A mother, cornered by a big cat, chooses to sacrifice her life to save her son. Why would she do this? (Read Isaiah 49:15.)

2. At the beginning, Manny, the woolly mammoth, seems not to want any company. Is this a good attitude to have? (Read 1 Peter 4:9.)

3. Sid, the silly-looking sloth, can be irritating, but he is the first one to decide that the baby needs to be returned to his "herd" (family), and he is willing to take a risk to do so. What does this say about judging someone based only on his looks or manners? (Read 1 Samuel 16:7.)

4. Later in the movie, we learn why Manny is a loner. He seems to have a reason to hate humans, yet he is trying to save a human baby.

Why? (Read Matthew 18:23-35.) Compare this to Soto's attitude toward humans.

5. Manny puts his life in danger to save Diego from certain death. What does this say about Manny's character? (Read John 15:13.) When Diego asks him why he did this, Manny says, "That's what you do in a herd." How could you apply this to your family? To other people, like kids at school?

6. At first Diego is a sneaky, lying cat who plans to betray Manny, Sid, and the baby to curry favor with the leader of the pack, Soto. By the end of the movie, he fights to protect them—from Soto. What causes this change of heart? (Read Colossians 3:12.)

7. When the human hunters first see Manny approaching, they take up their spears to attack, but the father of the baby senses something different about the mammoth and holds them back. What can we learn from that attitude? (Read Psalm 103:8.)

Follow-Up Activities
Bearing One Another's Burdens

Something that's too heavy for one person to carry can be carried by many. Example from the movie: Manny, Sid, and Diego must work together to save the baby from Soto's pack.

Fill a two-handled duffel bag with old newspapers or magazines until it is too heavy for one child to carry. Ask a child to try to carry it up some stairs or a certain distance across the room. If you have more than one child, have another help until you "run out" of children. Otherwise, help the child yourself.

Ask your kids these questions: Why couldn't you carry the bag by yourself? (It was too heavy.) What happened when others helped? (It got easier as more people helped.)

Read Galatians 6:2 and discuss ways to bear one another's burdens as a family. Remind your children that you—and God—are always there to help.

Protecting Others

In the movie Diego learns to protect others. Ask your child, "Who is a protector in our family?" (Mom, Dad, maybe a big sister or brother)

Your child can learn what it means to be a protector too. Give him or her a fragile item such as a raw egg. The object is to carry it around all day without breaking or losing it. The child must keep the item with him at all times—not put it down someplace. (This might work best on a weekend, a holiday, or during the summer when your child is out of school.) At the end of the day, ask these questions: What kinds of problems did you have protecting your egg? Did you get tired of keeping it with you at all times? What were the fun parts of protecting your egg? Besides family members, who else protects us? (God) Talk about how a protector loves and cares for the family, and discuss the responsibilities and joys of protecting others.

—Tom Neven

Iron Will

Rated: PG
Themes: Persevering in pursuit of an important goal, even in the face of great difficulty; competing fairly; love of family
Running Time: 1 hour, 49 minutes
Starring: Mackenzie Astin as Will Stoneman, Kevin Spacey as Harry Kingsley, David Ogden Stiers as J. W. Harper, Brian Cox as Angus McTeague, Penelope Windust as Mom (Maggie) Stoneman, August Schellenberg as Ned Dodd
Directed by: Charles Haid

Cautions

Even though this movie is rated PG, there are more than a few profanities, so you may want to tape this off of network television or use a filtering device. There are some scenes of violence. Will's father accidentally drowns. A pack of dogs turns on their cruel and abusive master, which might be frightening for younger viewers—especially if they're afraid of dogs. Men gamble over the outcome of the race, and there's a good bit of drinking and smoking in several scenes.

Story Summary

Will Stoneman, a 17-year-old living on the family farm out-side Birch Ridge, South Dakota, loves to race in his dogsled and has dreams of going to college. "Don't let fear stand in the way of your dream, Son," his father tells him. But when his dad dies in a drowning accident, Will's dream appears to die, too, and he and his mother are left with large debts that seemingly can only be repaid by selling the farm.

Will finds an application for a 522-mile-long dogsled race and surmises that his dad was going to enter the race. The $10,000 prize would be enough to pay off the family's debts and also pay for Will's college education. Will believes he can do it, though others think he doesn't have enough strength or experience for such an arduous task. Against his mother's better judgment, he enters the race.

Ned, a family friend who helps out on the farm, agrees to train Will. He begins a rigorous training program to help Will prepare for sleep deprivation, frostbite, hunger, constant running, and the obstacles of nature. But none of these is as formidable as the hardened racers Will must compete against.

When Will arrives at the starting point, he meets Harry Kingsley, a newspaper reporter who's fallen out of the good graces of his paper. Seeking a way to redeem his reputation and keep his job, he recognizes a story in Will Stoneman's reasons for entering the race. At first Kingsley is only interested in Will for his own purposes, but over time he begins to genuinely care about Will and admire his determination and integrity.

By running longer and sleeping less than the other racers, Will manages to take the lead. Fans across the country follow his progress in the week-long race in their daily newspapers. Overcoming terrible cold, a ruthless and cheating competitor, his own strategic mistakes, and his fear of racing alongside any body of water (because of his dad's drowning), Will earns the nickname Iron Will. At the end, in a sprint to the finish line against another racer, Will just barely manages to win.

Before You Watch

Point out that this tale, which is based on a true story, takes place back in 1917—almost 100 years ago. Several references are made to the idea that the United States might soon be at war against someone called "The Kaiser" (Kaiser Wilhelm II of Germany). Tell your child that, unfortunately, that did happen. World War I had been going on in Europe and the Middle East since 1914, and U.S. troops would enter the conflict just a few months after the race depicted in this film. Add that it's comforting to know that even in difficult times, there are "good news" events like this story taking place.

Bible Bookmarks

Leviticus 19:35-36; Joshua 1:9; Luke 12:15; Philippians 4:4-7; Hebrews 12:1; James 1:2-4

Talking Points

1. What were Will Stoneman's original reasons for wanting to enter the race? Toward the end, what does he give as his reason for staying in the race and trying to win?

2. When Angus McTeague offers Will first $3,000 then $5,000 to quit the race, what reason does Will give for not quitting? Would he have been wrong to take the money? (Read Exodus 23:8.)

3. What did you think of newspaper reporter Harry Kingsley at the start of the race? Did your opinion of him change by the end? Why or why not?

4. What reasons does railroad owner and race sponsor J. W. Harper give for allowing Will to enter and then stay in the race?

5. Ned Dodd tells Will that he has to earn the respect of the new lead dog in his team. What does Will do to merit that respect?

6. Why do you think people came out to watch Will and his team go by their towns?

7. While the Bible does not specifically address gambling, it does say much about the attitudes attached to gambling. (Read Luke 12:15, 1 Timothy 6:10, and James 4:1-3.) How does Mr. McTeague display greed and covetousness? (Money is more important to him than Will's safety.)

8. As Will is training for the race, Ned Dodd tells him, "When you come to face the thing you fear, let the Creator guide you." Later, toward the end of the race, when Will does face such a situation, he remembers Ned's words and takes courage. God has indeed promised to be with us in our most challenging moments. Look up and read aloud the following

passages: Joshua 1:9, Jeremiah 1:8, Matthew 6:25-33, and Philippians 4:4-7.

9. Lots of people think Will can't win because he is young and inexperienced. Name a person in the Bible who was young but did something great (David, Jesus, Samuel, Daniel, Miriam, Joash, among others).

 ## Follow-Up Activities

Pop Quiz

1. How long is the race that Will wins?
a) 1,000 miles
b) 50 miles
c) 522 miles

2. The race starts and finishes in which cities?
a) Starts in Nome, Alaska; finishes in Seattle, Washington
b) Starts in Montreal, Canada; finishes in Birch Ridge, South Dakota
c) Starts in Winnipeg, Canada; finishes in St. Paul, Minnesota

3. What's the name of Will's dad's lead dog, who then becomes Will's lead dog?
a) Charley
b) Gus
c) Sam

4. What's the prize for winning the race?
a) $10,000
b) $100,000
c) $1 million

Cheater, Cheater

Play a board or card game with your child. After a short time, cheat in a very obvious way so your child quickly catches on. When he or she protests, say, "How did you feel when I cheated you? Why?"

The wealthy businessmen sponsoring the race wager large amounts of money on the outcome. One of them (Angus McTeague), in his determination to win his bets, recruits a racer to cheat and even to use violence to keep Will from winning the contest. Ask, "In the movie, who cheats? Why does he cheat? What happens because he cheats?" Point out that it's often tempting to cheat—in school, in a game, at work—especially when you've got a lot at stake.

Ask your child, "Why is cheating wrong?" Then ask, "What are the likely consequences (what might happen) when we get caught cheating?" (We can get a bad grade if we cheat on a test. Others won't trust us anymore. We can get thrown out of a game or contest. Someone may get hurt.)

Next ask, "Who knows about our cheating even if no one else finds out?" Finally ask, "How does God feel about cheating?" For one example, specifically in the context of cheating in business, have your child look up and read aloud Leviticus 19:35-36.

—Larry Weeden

Jimmy Neutron: Boy Genius

Rated: G
Themes: Honesty, obeying parents, overcoming fears
Running Time: 1 hour, 22 minutes
Starring: The voices of Debi Derryberry as Jimmy Neutron, Rob Paulson as Carl, Patrick Stewart as King Goobot, Martin Short as Ooblar, Megan Cavanagh as Mom, Mark Decarlo as Dad, and Carolyn Lawrence as Cindy
Directed by: John A. Davis

Cautions

There are several uses of "kick their buttocks" and its variants. Nick, the "cool kid," calls the others "dweebs" because they won't lie to their parents. A pilot says, "Holy cow pies!" Jimmy more or less endorses evolution, comparing humans to monkeys. The Yokians, evil aliens, worship a giant, three-eyed chicken god called Poultra and plan to sacrifice all the parents to it. The soundtrack features songs by boy bands N'Sync and The Backstreet Boys, whose members have moved on to less wholesome activities. (N'Sync member Justin Timberlake was in the infamous Super Bowl XXXVIII halftime show.) Cindy does Tai Chi in a couple of scenes.

Story Summary

Jimmy Neutron exemplifies the term "boy genius" with his numerous gadgets, which include dressing, bed-making, and shoe-tying robots; a jet backpack; and his amazing robotic dog, Goddard.

As the story opens, Jimmy and his best friend, Carl, are hurtling through space in Jimmy's homemade rocket. Jimmy launches a message into space welcoming aliens and giving them coordinates for finding Earth.

Back home on Earth, Jimmy learns that Retroville's new amusement park, Retroland, will be opening that night. He wants nothing more than to attend the grand opening, but Mom and Dad say no because it's a school night. His mom says maybe they'll go next weekend, but that's not soon enough for Jimmy. He wishes there were no parents to ruin kids' fun, and Nick, the "cool kid," convinces Jimmy that he'll be cool too if he sneaks out of the house.

When Jimmy's parents ground him, he takes Nick's advice to sneak out and joins the other kids at Retroland. He makes it look like he's in bed by leaving Goddard under the covers. His parents come in to say good night and tell Jimmy that they love him, and Goddard records the conversation.

While all the kids are away at the theme park, the evil Yokians (gooey, green, egg-shaped aliens) land in Retroville and kidnap all the parents—including Jimmy's. Meanwhile the kids are having a great time at the park. When they see a shooting star, Carl says they can wish on it. Jimmy says, "I know what I'd wish for—I'd wish for no more parents. That way we could do whatever we wanted, whenever we wanted. We'd be free. We could have fun all the time!"

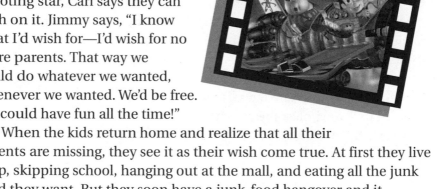

When the kids return home and realize that all their parents are missing, they see it as their wish come true. At first they live it up, skipping school, hanging out at the mall, and eating all the junk food they want. But they soon have a junk-food hangover and it becomes clear that they really miss—and need—their parents.

Jimmy goes home to find his parents, but there's no sign of them. He examines the note telling him they've gone on vacation. "What kind of parents take off and leave their kid? And they didn't even say good-bye," he muses. Goddard plays the recording of Jimmy's parents' bedtime visit, and Jimmy realizes that they said they'd see him in the morning.

They wouldn't have left—on vacation, no less—if they'd planned to see him in the morning. He goes to the lab and examines the notes supposedly left by all the parents. They're fakes.

The kids all come to Jimmy for help. It's up to Jimmy's brain and his friends to get their parents back. Jimmy turns all the amusement park rides into spaceships, and the kids of Retroville travel to Yokia to battle the Yokians, who worship a giant, three-eyed god that resembles a chicken: Poultra. It seems the parents are intended to be living sacrifices to the chicken god.

The Yokians round up and jail the kids. Frightened and missing their parents, the kids turn against Jimmy when they find out that the coordinates he sent into space enabled the Yokians to find Earth. But Cindy comes to Jimmy's defense and tells him that the kids are just scared and talks him into trying to free their parents. "There are a bunch of kids in here who need you," she says. "I do too." Jimmy calls Goddard, who blows up the jail bars so all the kids can escape. While the other kids keep the guards busy, Jimmy frees the parents, and Sheen gets the ship ready to escape.

With kids and parents aboard, they take off but are pursued by the Yokians. Finally, they defeat the other ships and only King Goobot's ship is left. When the king insults Jimmy, Jimmy goes out into space, uses a gadget to make himself "planet size," and blows the king's ship away.

Back onboard his own ship, Jimmy finds his parents and apologizes, and they tell him how proud they are of him. When the earthlings arrive back home, things get back to normal with one exception—the kids now realize they need and want their parents and their parents love them and want what's best for them.

 ## Before You Watch

Jimmy's full name is James Isaac Neutron. Explain the play on words with Isaac Newton and why Newton, a devout Christian, is important to modern science.

Bible Bookmarks

Colossians 3:20; Exodus 20:3; Luke 12:48b; 1 Samuel 16:7

Talking Points

1. Jimmy's teacher is portrayed as mean. Do kids owe obedience to teachers, even mean ones, as they do their parents? (Read Romans 13:1-5, but also Acts 5:29.)

2. Jimmy's inventions wreck the neighborhood, set his house's curtains on fire, and shrink his teacher. Jimmy obviously has been given a great gift of intelligence. Are these examples the best way to use it? (Read Luke 12:48b.)

3. Even though he's told he can't go to the Retroland Amusement Park, Jimmy sneaks out anyway. He also wishes there were no more parents so he'd be free to have fun all the time. Why is this wrong? (Read Colossians 3:20.)

4. Jimmy creates a girl-eating plant, and there is quite a bit of rivalry between Jimmy and Cindy. Is this the right way for boys and girls to treat each other? (Read 1 Peter 2:17.)

5. Nick is the "cool kid" who looks down on others. What should our attitude be to everyone? (Read 1 Samuel 16:7.)

6. The Yokians worship a huge, man-eating chicken god called Poultra. What does the Bible say about worshipping anyone or anything other than God? (Read Exodus 20:1-3.) Poultra doesn't seem to be the kind of god we'd like to have. Why is this? (Read Deuteronomy 4:31.)

7. At the end of the movie Jimmy apologizes to his parents and says, "I thought I was smart enough to do everything on my own—that I didn't need you." Have you ever thought the same thing? Talk about a time when a smart idea turned out to be not so smart. (Parents can share stories too.)

Follow-Up Activity

Obeying Your Parents

Parents love their children and want what's best for them, even though that may sometimes seem to spoil the fun. Example from the movie: Jimmy lies to his parents and sneaks out of the house because he doesn't want to wait until the weekend to visit Retroland.

Build a maze using long strips of cloth, yarn, or string. Blindfold your child and tell him to do *exactly* what a parent tells him—for example, two steps forward and then turn left. Start with a parent giving the instructions, but then have someone else periodically give a wrong direction that will cause him to wander off course.

Ask your kids these questions: What happened when you listened to someone other than your parents? (You went in the wrong direction.) Why is it important to listen carefully to your parents and obey them? (They have more experience and want to help you.)

Read Colossians 3:20. Discuss with your kids ways to obey you and what happens when they disobey.

Just for Fun

Patrick Stewart plays the voice of Yokian King Goobot. He is a Shakespearian actor known for his many serious roles, including Captain Jean-Luc Picard on *Star Trek: Next Generation*. Compare those roles to the silly, hysterical character he plays in this movie.

Jimmy's robot dog is named Goddard after Robert H. Goddard, an American physicist and considered the father of America's space program.

—*Tom Neven*

The Lion, the Witch and the Wardrobe (1988, BBC)

Rated: NR
Themes: Repentance, faith, trust, loyalty, love between brothers and sisters, courage, honesty, jealousy, mercy, selflessness, truthfulness
Starring: Richard Dempsey as Peter, Sophie Cook as Susan, Jonathan R. Scott as Edmund, Sophie Wilcox as Lucy, Barbara Kellerman as the White Witch, and Michael Aldridge as the Professor
Based on the book by C. S. Lewis
Running Time: 2 hours, 49 minutes
Directed by: Marilyn Fox

Cautions

Narnia is a land populated by talking animals, mythical creatures, and a witch. Also, the scenes featuring the witch can be rather intense. Because she is the embodiment of pure evil, she lacks all humanity and exudes a kind of primal noxiousness. The sacrifice of Aslan is especially intense, as is the battle scene near the end of the movie. All in all, this is probably not suitable for younger children.

Story Summary

Visiting the English countryside during World War II to escape the bombing of London, the Pevensie children—Peter, Susan, Edmund, and Lucy—stay at the house of a professor-friend of the family. One rainy day they play hide-and-seek, and Lucy, the youngest, strays into the land of Narnia through a magic wardrobe. There she meets Mr. Tumnus, a Faun—a mythical creature, half-goat and half-man. She goes home with him for tea and learns of the cruel White Witch who rules Narnia, where it is always winter and never Christmas. All the creatures there are under the power of the White Witch. After a couple of hours, Lucy returns to her world through the wardrobe.

She excitedly tells the others about her adventures and leads them to the wardrobe, but it's no longer magic. The others think Lucy is either kidding or crazy. Edmund is especially mean to her.

The children play hide-and-seek on the next rainy day. Edmund follows Lucy to the wardrobe and, to his surprise, finds himself in Narnia. Separated from Lucy, he sets out along a road, where a beautiful womanlike creature appears. She asks, "Are you a Son of Adam?" He says that he is human. She offers Edmund some candy called Turkish delight, which he wolfs down, making him rather sick. After stuffing himself, he begs for more, which she promises on condition that he bring the other children to her. He agrees, and she lets him go. Edmund runs into Lucy, and they return together through the wardrobe.

Back in our world, Peter and Susan encounter Lucy and Edmund just returning from Narnia. Lucy is thrilled that Edmund also got in. But Edmund lies about his being there, and Lucy feels betrayed. Peter and Susan, worried about Lucy, go see the professor. After he hears their story, he concludes Lucy is probably telling the truth.

Soon, the children are forced to flee to the wardrobe as some elderly house guests invade their privacy. They are astonished to find themselves in Narnia. Immediately they meet Mr. Beaver, who takes them to his house where they're fed and told about a new development—Aslan is on the move.

Edmund sneaks away. Mr. Beaver knows what's happened: He's gone to the witch. Afraid that Edmund will tell her where they are and that she'll come after them, they head for the Stone Table. Meanwhile, Edmund has made his way to the witch's castle. She is furious that he has not brought the other children to her. He blurts out where they are going, betraying them. The witch and her minions head to the Stone Table.

When the children arrive, there is a surprise awaiting them: Aslan has arrived. He asks some of the mythical beasts loyal to him to free Edmund from the witch's clutches. They bring him to Aslan, who restores him to fellowship with his brother and sisters.

Soon, the White Witch arrives, asking for a parlay with Aslan. He agrees, and she declares that since Edmund betrayed his brother and sisters, he has violated the laws of the Old Magic and is hers to slay, if she chooses. Aslan agrees that by the terms of the Old Magic, Edmund is truly hers to do with as she wishes. But he requests a private conference. They confer, and return in agreement. Edmund is free to go. But a price must still be paid.

That night, the girls can't sleep. They follow Aslan. They ask if they can come along and he agrees, so long as they remain hidden and stop following him when he says to. He makes his way down to the Stone Table, where the witch has summoned all kinds of malignant creatures who cavort about. The White Witch orders Aslan bound and muzzled, and he submits to her power. She declares that he has lost. She tells him his death will be for naught, for what is to prevent her from slaying Edmund as well after he is dead? She plunges the knife into him, even as the children watch, horrified.

In the morning, the girls go to see if they can attend to Aslan. He stirs, arises, and appears to be perfectly okay. The girls don't understand, until Aslan tells them that there is a magic even older than the Old Magic. It decrees that if a blameless one offers himself for the life of the guilty, he will not stay dead but will arise and live again.

Aslan seeks out the White Witch, who has been preparing for war against all Narnia. As the battle begins, he casts her down, even as her forces are attacking the good creatures of Narnia. After a fierce battle, the forces of good prevail, with the Pevensie children employing special gifts they've been given by Aslan. Then, according to prophecy, they are crowned the four rulers of Narnia at Cair Paravel, where they enjoy a long and happy rule.

One day, as they are out riding, they come across a curious sight: a lamppost out in the middle of nowhere. They investigate, find the wardrobe, and re-emerge into our world just as the elderly house guests are leaving. Though the children have been in Narnia for many years, scarcely minutes have gone by in our world.

Before You Watch

You might want to read *The Lion, the Witch and the Wardrobe,* and perhaps others in the "Chronicles of Narnia" series, before watching the film version. The entire series is also available on CD from Focus on the Family Radio Theatre. (Call 1-800-932-9123 or check you local bookstore.)

Bible Bookmarks

Romans 3:23-24; 1 Thessalonians 5:22; 2 Timothy 2:22

Talking Points

1. Can you recount all of Edmund's wrong actions that lead up to his becoming a slave to the White Witch? Do the other children in any way contribute to Edmund's bad behavior? If so, how? Is there any one particular action that sets Edmund on a path to enslavement, or is it more like a slippery slope with many smaller actions?

2. When Edmund first encounters the White Witch, she offers him food and drink. Is there some special significance in his eating the witch's food? What do you think would have happened to Edmund if he had politely declined the witch's food? Do you think the White Witch would have had any real power over Edmund if he had not cooperated with her? What does the Bible say we should do when we encounter evil? (See 1 Thessalonians 5:22, 2 Timothy 2:22.)

3. After Lucy returns from Narnia the second time, she is relieved that Edmund will be able to back up her story. Instead, he lies and tells Peter and Susan that Lucy's making it all up. What effect does this have on Lucy? On Edmund himself? On Peter and Susan?

4. The two older children are so upset by these events they ask the professor for help. After they explain what has happened, the professor responds unexpectedly. What does he say? What are the only three possibilities he suggests?

5. Aslan, the king of the beasts, is the rightful ruler of Narnia; the White Witch is a usurper (one who takes by force and without right). What begins to happen when Aslan first returns to his kingdom? What does it mean when the animals talk about Aslan being "not a tame lion"?

6. When the White Witch comes to parlay with Aslan, she declares that by the laws laid down long ago, Edmund rightfully belongs to her. Is she right? How does Aslan's sacrifice free Edmund?

7. How does Aslan finally defeat the White Witch?

8. In what ways is Aslan like Jesus?

Follow-Up Activity

"Kid's Kingdom" Game

Have a coronation ceremony, crowning your kids kings and queens of Narnia. Give them robes, scepters, and crowns. Set up chairs as thrones (one for each child in the family) and have them rule in the following cases, describing how they would handle each. (Feel free to make up additional situations for your royal rulers.)

1. Some of the woodland animals complain about the White Witch's former henchmen, the dwarfs. They are bad neighbors, always leaving trash around and making a racket.

2. A baby mouse dies and the family asks you to attend the funeral. You want to, but Lucy thinks baby mice die a lot and if you went to every animal's funeral, you would never have time for anything else.

3. Though he has already made a public apology, a group of badgers is calling for one of your co-leaders, Edmund, to be dethroned for his involvement with the White Witch.

—Jan P. Dennis

Little Secrets

Rated: PG
Themes: The difference between keeping secrets and telling lies, being trustworthy, friendship, hard work, importance of family, being authentic, confessing mistakes, forgiving mistakes, acceptance, setting worthy goals
Running Time: 1 hour, 36 minutes
Starring: Evan Rachel Wood as Emily, Michael Angarano as Philip, David Gallagher as David, Vivica A. Fox as Pauline, Jan Broberg Felt as Caroline Lindstrom, Rick Macy as Eddie Lindstrom, Haley McCormick as Jenny, and RuDee Lipscomb as Laurel
Directed by: Blair Treu

Cautions

A kid is stealing from his dad and a store, but Emily advises him to confess and make it right. Fifteen-year-old David is in a drunk-driving accident involving some underage drinkers. The action happens offscreen and is a pivotal event in his growth.

Story Summary

Everyone has a secret . . . and almost everyone in the neighborhood confides in 14-year-old Emily. Secrets are very important to Emily because she has a few of her own.

Emily is an aspiring concert violinist who also runs a small business on the side. On Wednesdays from 2:30-4:30, for 50 cents, she listens to the children of the neighborhood confess their secrets. For example, Gregory is learning the "joys" of stealing—first as he steals from his father's wallet, then from the store. Isabelle is writing notes to her older sister's new beau on the Internet while her sister is away at camp. Lea is collecting cats even though her sister is allergic to them. The children love Emily because she listens and keeps their secrets. They bring her all the things they've broken and she puts them in labeled lunch bags, which she locks in a trunk in her old playhouse.

When she's not listening to secrets, Emily is practicing her violin. She is so dedicated to her aspirations of becoming a concert violinist that she practices every spare moment. She even remains home instead of going to summer camp with her two best friends, Jenny and Laurel, because she has an important audition coming up. She takes private lessons from Pauline and plays along with televised symphonies. It is through this quirk that she meets the new neighbors and befriends 12-year-old Philip, who becomes her summer buddy.

Emily is distraught over her 40+-year-old mother's pregnancy. She resents the coming baby and is obviously fearful that her parents will love the baby more than they do her. This seems a little out of place until we later learn one of Emily's best-kept secrets. Due to Emily's obvious distress over the coming baby, her parents decide they will each share a secret with her—something no one else knows, not even each other. Emily's mother takes her to the ultrasound appointment where the baby's sex will be revealed. Her father sits on the roof with her (Emily's favorite place to play the violin) and shares how frightened he is of becoming a father again at age 50.

Emily struggles with a bit of self-righteousness, and her perfectionist tendencies sometimes make it hard to forgive others their faults. When David, Philip's 15-year-old brother, is kicked out of tennis camp for his involvement in a drunk-driving accident (he was not driving, but he did drink one beer), Emily finds it impossible to befriend him.

The secrets Emily must keep finally get out of hand. Emily struggles—not with keeping the secrets, for she will never change her ethics, but the secrets weigh too heavily on her when she realizes that they are hurting others. Stressed by the upcoming competition, the secrets, her strained relationships, and the coming baby, she closes down her secrets booth and goes "on vacation." The neighborhood children are angry with her unavailability and turn against her. Seeing a business opportunity, Philip sets up his own secrets booth.

Finally, Pauline, Emily's violin teacher, wants to share her secret with Emily, but Emily doesn't want to hear any more secrets. Pauline shares anyway, telling Emily that "Secrets hurt. . . . You can't keep secrets about yourself and lead a true life. And you shouldn't encourage others to do the same." This is a pivotal point for Emily because she admires Pauline so much and has looked up to her as a role model. Pauline's confession helps Emily begin to realize that even those who have highly admirable qualities are not perfect, yet we can still love and respect them.

When Emily falls off the roof and is admitted to the hospital, Philip breaks the cycle of secrets by confessing that he broke the knight from his parents' antique chess set. Emily has to miss her audition, but David and Philip have an idea: They will go to Symphony Hall with a tape she made for Laurel and Jenny over the summer.

When her friends visit the hospital, Emily confesses her big secret: Her parents were killed in a drunk-driving accident when she was 10 months old and she was adopted by the Lindstroms. Her confession is a wake-up call for David and he sees the devastation that drinking and driving can cause. He promises that he will never do it again.

When Emily gets out of the hospital, she opens her secrets business one last time. She gives the neighborhood children a refund on all the secrets she's kept and tells them to take back the things they've broken, go home, and tell their parents the truth. Emily is now out of business for good, but the truth has transformed the neighborhood.

Before You Watch

Look up the words *secret* and *lie* in the dictionary. Ask your kids, "Can a secret ever be a lie?" (Yes, if a secret is meant to deceive someone.) Tell them to look for some secrets that are also lies in the movie.

Bible Bookmarks
Proverbs 11:13; 2 Corinthians 4:2; Matthew 5:33-35

Talking Points
1. Read these verses about keeping secrets: Psalm 44:21 and Psalm 90:8. What does the Bible say about keeping secrets from God?

2. When you break something by accident, what do you do? How do you feel about what you do? How do you feel when you confess to the owner of the object you broke?

3. What is the difference between a secret that should be told and a secret that should be kept? What is the difference between a secret and a lie?

4. What do you do when someone tells you a secret? Do you keep it forever? Or do you keep it until you can't stand it anymore and then tell someone? Or do you tell right away? How does your choice make you feel?

5. Talk about these three things Emily says: "I know all this stuff I can't stand knowing." "I told something I swore I never would." "I have a secret no one even knows about." Read Matthew 5:33-35 and Leviticus 5:4 to see what God says about giving your word (swearing) to do something.

6. David says, "If you want to be close to someone, you can't keep secrets from them." Do you think he's correct? Are the people you feel closest to ones who share secrets with you or ones who keep secrets from you?

7. Emily's big secret involves her adoption. Why do you think she doesn't want anyone to know she is adopted? How does she feel after she tells her friends she is adopted?

8. Emily is very angry with David when she finds out that he drank a beer and went driving with the other boys. Do you think she should have forgiven him? Why or why not? Have you ever had to forgive someone for doing something very wrong or hurtful? Has someone ever had to forgive you? How did it feel to forgive? How did it feel to be forgiven?

Follow-Up Activities
Two Truths and a Lie
Tell each other three things: two true things, and one lie. Have everyone guess which is the lie. How did you feel when you told

the lie? After everyone has had a turn, look up Proverbs 12:22 and John 8:32 and discuss why it's right to always tell the truth.

Samson's Secret
Read the story of Samson in Judges 13:1-5 and 16:4-30. What secret should he have kept? What made him tell his secret? What happened because he didn't keep the secret?

Telephone
Have everyone sit in a circle on the floor. (If your family is small, you may want to play this when your child has friends over.) One person will whisper a secret to the next person, which each family member or friend will in turn pass. The last person to hear the secret will tell it aloud. How has the secret changed? Talk about how passing "secrets" can sometimes distort the truth. Look up the word *gossip* in the dictionary and talk about how gossip can hurt people.

—*Lissa Halls Johnson*

Miracle on 34th Street (1947)

Rated: NR
Themes: Believing in people, the pleasure and value of imagination, not letting Christmas become commercialized
Running Time: 1 hour, 37 minutes
Starring: Maureen O'Hara as Doris Walker, John Payne as Fred Gailey, Edmund Gwenn as Kris Kringle, Natalie Wood as Susan Walker
Directed by: George Seaton

Cautions

Parents who don't want their children to believe in Santa should probably avoid this film. The man who is originally hired to play Santa in the parade is severely inebriated, but Kris lets him know his behavior is shameful. Mr. Shellhammer tells Doris he'll mix double-strength martinis that evening so his wife will agree to let Kris stay at their home. Indeed, Mrs. Shellhammer is drunk when the call comes.

Story Summary

The story begins as an old, white-bearded man who identifies himself as Kris Kringle steps in at the last minute to play Santa Claus in the annual Macy's Thanksgiving Day parade. Mrs. Walker, a Macy's employee who organizes the parade, then hires Kris to be the in-store Santa as the Christmas shopping season begins.

Kris soon surprises everyone, especially his employers, by recommending that parents go to other stores when Macy's doesn't have the toys their kids want. He even tells shoppers which store has the lowest price on any particular toy. Mr. Macy starts receiving letters and telegrams thanking the store for being so bighearted and putting the interests of the children first, and he decides to make recommending other stores a storewide policy. Kris is also kind and wise, and he becomes extremely popular. Surprisingly, he speaks to the children in a number of languages—including sign language.

Mrs. Walker and her daughter, Susan, along with their neighbor Mr. Gailey, befriend Kris. Susan tells Mr. Gailey that she doesn't believe in Santa Claus. In fact, her mother does not tell her fairy tales at all because she thinks they're silly. When Mr. Gailey takes Susan to see Kris at Macy's, Mrs. Walker confronts him about encouraging Susan to believe in Santa Claus, telling him it will set up a harmful mental conflict within Susan. "Who is she going to believe?" she asks.

Susan has a secret wish: She wants a home in the country for herself and her mom—complete with a swing in the backyard. She shows Kris a picture of her dream house, but tells him she knows he can't get her the house because there's no such thing as Santa Claus. He tells her it's a tall order, but he'll see what he can do.

Meanwhile, back at the store, Macy's staff psychologist takes a strong disliking to Kris. And when Kris insists that he's the real Santa Claus, the psychologist has Kris taken to the mental hospital for an exam. Because he feels that his friends don't believe in him, Kris purposely fails the exam and is found insane.

Mr. Gailey then assures Kris that his friends haven't deserted him, and Kris is ready to go home. But first, because of the failed exam, he has to go through a court hearing to determine if he should be committed to an institution for the insane. Mr. Gailey represents Kris in the hearing, and they prevail when Mr. Gailey shows that the U.S. Postal Service, by delivering mail addressed to "Santa" to Kris at the courthouse, believes him to be the true Santa. Kris is free to make his annual Christmas Eve rounds.

Kris has one last gift to give, though. On Christmas morning Mrs. Walker, Susan, and Mr. Gailey visit Kris at the Brooks Home—the "old folks home" where he normally lives. As they are leaving, Kris gives Mr. Gailey directions for a "shortcut" home. Susan is dejected because she didn't get the big present she wanted for Christmas. On the way home, she suddenly spies a house that looks very familiar. No, it couldn't be. She orders Mr. Gailey to stop the car, gets out, and runs into the house. Her mother follows, saying she can't just go into a stranger's house. But inside Susan finds it's exactly what she had asked for in a home. She recognizes her room—and there's even a swing in the backyard.

The house is empty, of course, and Mr. Gailey tells Doris that it's for sale. It looks as if Susan will get her Christmas wish after all.

Before You Watch

Tell your child that in this movie, the Macy's department store will adopt an unusual policy for a retail business. But it's actually a policy consistent with Jesus' words in Luke 6:31: "Do to others as you would have them do to you." Encourage them to look for what that policy is as they watch the film.

Bible Bookmarks

Luke 6:31; Proverbs 14:21; Galatians 5:22

Talking Points

1. What is Kris Kringle's big concern about what has become of Christmas?

2. What does Mrs. Walker believe about fantasy and imagination? Why do you think she holds that opinion?

3. Why do you think the store psychologist dislikes Kris so much?

4. What is that store policy that's consistent with Jesus' instruction in Luke 6:31, known as the Golden Rule? What are Mr. Macy's motives in making it a storewide policy?

5. What's the one really big thing about Christmas that's missing from this movie? (Jesus and His birth)

6. How does our family do at keeping Jesus in His rightful place at the center of our celebrating?

7. What else could we do to honor Jesus in His birthday season?

 ## Follow-Up Activities

Pop Quiz

1. In what city does the story take place?
a) Philadelphia
b) St. Louis
c) New York

2. Macy's is what kind of store?
a) pet store
b) grocery store
c) department store

3. The story in *Miracle on 34th Street* takes place between which two holidays?
a) Valentine's Day and Easter
b) Thanksgiving and Christmas
c) Mother's Day and Father's Day

4. What does Mr. Gailey do for a living?
a) he's a dog catcher
b) he's a psychologist
c) he's a lawyer

Giving to Others

At Christmastime there are many ways your family can give to others in your community and around the world. You can give shoeboxes filled with practical goods and toys to needy children in developing countries through Operation Christmas Child (www.samaritanspurse.org) or give clothing and toys to children of prisoners through Angel Tree (www.angeltree.org). Your church, school, or place of employment may have a food, clothing, or toy drive. Choose one of these giving opportunities and involve the whole family by letting your children help select the gifts and contribute some of their own money.

Advent Celebration

Advent begins on the fourth Sunday before Christmas. Make an advent wreath with some greenery and candles to celebrate as a family. Gather to read scriptures, pray, sing Christmas carols, and eat traditional Christmas foods. (For more information about Advent traditions, consult a book from your library or bookstore, or check the Internet.)

Include this discussion about the movie in one of your Advent Sundays:

Toward the end of the movie, Mr. Gailey gives Doris Walker this definition of faith: "Faith is believing in things when common sense tells you not to." He's referring to the modern myth of Santa Claus as a man who lives at the North Pole and delivers presents all over the world on Christmas Eve, flying through the air in a reindeer-drawn sleigh. However, it's an understanding of faith that many people today would also apply to belief in God. Remind your child of what Mr. Gailey said, and then point out that faith in the Creator God and His Son, Jesus, is not only taught in the Bible, but it also "makes sense." You can refer to things like the clear reality of human sin and, therefore, our deserving punishment from a holy God, how only someone who had never sinned Himself could pay the price for our sins, how the God who created the universe out of nothing would surely have the power to create a baby in a virgin's womb and later raise Jesus from the dead, and so on.

—*Larry Weeden*

National Velvet

Rated: G
Themes: Courage, honesty, personal integrity, fair play, importance of family, second chances, value of hard work, proper use of resources, understanding of seasons
Running Time: 2 hours, 4 minutes
Starring: Elizabeth Taylor as Velvet Brown, Mickey Rooney as Mi Taylor, Anne Revere as Mrs. Brown, Donald Crisp as Mr. Brown, Angela Lansbury as Edwina Brown, Jackie "Butch" Jenkins as Donald Brown, and Juanita Quigley as Malvolia Brown
Directed by: Clarence Brown

Cautions

When Mi goes to London to enter Velvet's horse in the Grand National Steeplechase, he meets up with some old pals in a pub. Looking for an opportunity to fleece him of the entrance fee money he's carrying, they get him drunk. Since it provides a true test of character for Mi, this scene should not be skipped over, even though it shows Mi behaving badly. It will provide plenty of opportunities for discussion.

Story Summary

Velvet Brown, the daughter of a small-town English butcher, meets Mi Taylor, a young man traveling from town to town on foot. Together they watch a magnificent horse galloping in a nearby field. Velvet is immediately taken by the high-spirited horse, Pie, who has a tendency to jump out of his pasture. Velvet invites Mi to come have dinner at her house. Velvet's father, Mr. Brown, hires Mi to do odd jobs, even though he thinks Mi has a suspicious look about him.

When Pie escapes one time too many, his owner decides to raffle him off. Velvet is the winner and Pie is hers. It turns out that Mi has a background in training and riding horses, although there is some mystery about his past. After noticing that Velvet has a real way with horses, Mi agrees to begin training her and the horse. When Velvet hears about the Grand National Steeplechase, she asks Mi if he thinks her horse has a chance. Mi shrugs and says it would be a long shot—besides, there's a £100 entrance fee.

In a key scene, Velvet goes to her mother who begins reminiscing about her days as a championship swimmer—she was the first woman to swim the English Channel. She pulls out a purse filled with money and tells Velvet that she's been waiting for just the right time to use it.

When the time comes to pay the entrance fee, the Browns send Mi to London to pay it. Then comes the crucial scene in the pub. Meeting up with some old track buddies, Mi tells them of his good fortune and what he's thinking about doing with the £100—which doesn't include registering Pie for the Grand National. They concoct a plan to get him drunk and take the money. They succeed, and it looks as if Mi is going to slip back into his old ways. At the very last minute, though, he snatches back the purse of money and storms out of the pub.

Back at the Brown home, Mi and Velvet begin intense training. They're finally ready, and they leave early one morning for the Grand National. When they arrive at check-in, the jockey they hired to ride Pie can't do it, but they find another jockey whose horse had to scratch at the last minute. Velvet refuses to let him ride, though, because of his arrogance and disregard for Pie.

Meanwhile, the secret of Mi's past comes out. A jockey was killed in a race in which he was riding, and some blamed Mi for the accident. He has never ridden since, but he decides to put aside his fear and shame and ride in the Grand National the next day. But Velvet has already decided that *she* will ride Pie. Mi relents, and they enter Velvet as the jockey under the name of one of the jockeys they didn't use.

Race day is clear and beautiful. As the race begins, Pie and Velvet get a poor start and immediately fall back toward the rear of the pack. But it's a long course with 30 jumps, and gradually Pie and Velvet move up as many horses stumble and pile up. As they approach the end of the course there are only two horses to beat. Velvet urges Pie on, and they just nose out the favorite and win the Grand National Steeplechase.

But wait! Velvet falls off right after crossing the finish line. As she is taken to the local medical facility, her victory is challenged. She is examined; it is discovered she is a girl—and females are not permitted to ride in the Grand National. The challenge is upheld when officials find an obscure rule stating that jockeys must complete one circuit of the track after finishing the race. But meanwhile, it has been announced that the winner of the Grand National is a girl who has ridden an unknown horse. The English immediately take Velvet to heart, calling her their National Velvet, and even though she doesn't get to keep the prize money, she has won over all of England.

Back at home, offers begin pouring in from Hollywood. Velvet's father is ecstatic. But Velvet doesn't want that for Pie. And Mrs. Brown wonders if they really need a lot of money—hasn't that been the undoing of many families, and aren't they perfectly well-off? In the end, Mr. Brown sees that the happiness of his daughter—and indeed all the family—is more important than the chance at riches, and he is content with Velvet's decision.

Before You Watch

Ask your kids, "What if you had a chance to go to Hollywood to be in movies? Would you want to do that? Why or why not?" Talk about the good and bad sides of such an opportunity. Say, "We're going to see a movie about a girl who gets that chance. What do you think she will do? Let's watch the movie and see if you're right."

Bible Bookmarks
1 Corinthians 9:24-25; Ecclesiastes 3:1-8

Talking Points

1. When Mi Taylor first comes to the Brown home, there is suspicion on both sides; Mr. Brown suspects him of being untrustworthy, and Mi suspects that the Browns are just patronizing him. Mrs. Brown, however, seems to have a slightly different attitude. She has her doubts about Mi's character, but she also sees promise in him and wants to give him a chance to prove himself. She also is very concerned about being kind and hospitable to Mi. Why do the Browns distrust Mi? Is Mrs. Brown right to give him another chance? What does the Bible say about kindness to strangers and hospitality? (See 2 Kings 4:8-36 and Hebrews 13:2.)

2. In the scene at the pub, it looks as if Mi is going to revert to his old ways and either steal the entrance fee money or waste it on drinking. What makes him change his mind? Does it have anything to do with the treatment he has received from the Browns—with the trust they put in him to wisely use their money? What if Mi *had* wasted the money? Would that mean the Browns shouldn't have treated him as they did?

3. When Velvet returns home and sees all the offers to come to America and make a lot of money, what does she do? What do you think about her rejection of these offers? Would the money have made the family happier? Why or why not? What does the apostle Paul say about possessions (Philippians 4:11-12)?

4. In the next-to-last scene in the movie, as Mi is leaving, he and Mr. Brown have a chat. For the first time, Mr. Brown calls him Mi, instead of Boy or Lad. Mi asks him why. Mr. Brown replies that when he took him in, Mi had a suspicious look about him. Mi reveals that he almost took the entrance fee money. What are the reasons he gives for not taking it?

5. Mi also mentions that he hopes someone will think kindly of him after he's gone. Who is it? Do you think Mi has really changed, and if so, why?

Follow-Up Activities

A Time for Everything

Read Ecclesiastes 3:1-8. Divide your family into teams and have each team create a simple tune for these words. Perform your song for the other team(s) and let everyone vote for his or her favorite tune. Use the winning melody to memorize this Scripture passage.

If your family is not musical, try doing the text as a recitation. Award computer-generated certificates for recitations (best delivery, most unique style, clearest enunciation, best expression, and so on).

Chariots of Fire
In the movie *Chariots of Fire* the main character, Eric Liddell, says, "When I run, I feel His pleasure." Watch this movie together as a family, or just have a discussion about what Liddell's statement means. Is it really possible that God experiences joy when His creatures live up to their potential? See if your kids can think of similar instances when they've felt the pleasure of others for their accomplishments or they've expressed their own joy at a brother's or sister's success—or even a pet's achievement.

—Jan P. Dennis

Old Yeller

Rated: G
Themes: Selflessness and self-sacrifice; finding the good in bad situations; the importance of doing what's necessary, even when it's difficult
Running Time: 1 hour, 24 minutes
Starring: Tommy Kirk as Travis Coates, Dorothy McGuire as Katy Coates, Kevin Corcoran as Arliss Coates, Fess Parker as Jim Coates, Beverly Washburn as Lisbeth Searcy, Jeff York as Bud Searcy, and Chuck Connors as Burn Sanderson
Directed by: Robert Stevenson

Cautions

Arliss, the younger brother, is continually disrespectful and disobedient toward his mother; she always dismisses his words and behavior with the phrase "He's just a little boy." Some children will be upset when Travis has to shoot his dog, even though it's necessary and he's doing it out of love for his pet.

Story Summary

The Coates family lives on a Texas farm in the period shortly after the American Civil War. The dad has to go away for several months on a cattle drive to Kansas, leaving the mom in charge and the older son, Travis, as the "man of the house." A big, yellow dog (Old Yeller) soon shows up and causes trouble, but he wins the heart of the younger boy, Arliss.

At first Travis dislikes Yeller. The dog breaks down the fence, chases the mule, steals from the family's supply of meat, and generally makes a lot of extra work for the boy. When Travis complains to his mom, Mrs.

Coates tells Travis that any animal will steal food if it's hungry enough. But even Travis soon grows to love the brave and loyal dog, and when Lisbeth Searcy tells him she's seen Yeller steal meat, eggs, and cornbread from neighbors, he tells her he's going to keep the dog close to home.

Before long, Old Yeller is proving his worth. He protects the family from a mama bear after Arliss tries to catch her cub. He chases raccoons out of the cornfield. He saves Travis from a charging mama cow.

The boys nearly lose their beloved friend when a stranger, Mr. Sanderson, comes to claim his lost dog. But seeing how the boys love the dog, he trades Old Yeller for a horned toad and a home-cooked meal. Now Yeller is really theirs. As he's leaving the ranch, Mr. Sanderson warns Travis that there's a rabies plague in the area. He tells him to watch out for animals staggering around and slobbering.

Travis is gored in the leg when he tries to mark some javelinas and is attacked by the pack. Yeller comes to his rescue and is badly wounded. Mrs. Coates comes to sew up the dog's wounds, and together they take him back to the house to heal.

When the family's cow becomes sick, they recognize the signs of rabies and put her down. As Mrs. Coates and Lisbeth are burning the carcass, a wolf tries to attack and Yeller fights him off. Travis shoots the wolf, saving Yeller's life. But Mrs. Coates tells Travis that the wolf had to be rabid; no healthy wolf would come that close to a fire. She insists that Yeller be quarantined in a pen for one month to make sure he doesn't have rabies.

While Travis is laid up in bed with his leg wound, Lisbeth comes to visit and brings him a surprise—one of Old Yeller's puppies. She tells him the pup is part of Old Yeller. He tells her that he may be *part of* Old Yeller, but he *ain't* Old Yeller. Lisbeth's feelings are hurt and she gives the pup to Arliss.

The family watches Yeller closely for several weeks, hoping he'll be okay. But eventually it becomes clear that he has grown sick beyond hope of recovery and must be put down to end his suffering.

Mr. Coates returns home just as Travis, brokenhearted, is burying the dog. After hearing the story from his wife, he goes to find Travis and talks with him about life's hard realities, but also about the fact that "there's also a lot that's mighty fine." As a rule, he tells Travis, you can find something good to replace precious things that have been lost (in this case, Old Yeller's puppy).

Before You Watch

Read John 15:13 to your child: "Greater love has no one than this, that he lay down his life for his friends." Talk briefly about how this scripture encourages us to give of ourselves in general and, in the extreme if need be, to even give our lives to protect those we love. Then suggest, "As we watch the movie, let's look for examples of this verse being lived out."

Bible Bookmarks

John 15:13; Ephesians 6:1-3

Talking Points

1. Why do you think Old Yeller was always quick to put himself at risk to defend the Coates family?

2. How would you like to have a younger brother like Arliss? Why? How would you like to have an older brother like Travis? Why? Do you ever act like Arliss? Ask your mom or dad if you're right.

3. How did Travis usually treat Lisbeth Searcy? How did that make her feel?

4. What did Mr. Coates tell Travis at the end of the movie about how to respond when life "knocks you flat on the ground"? When have we seen something good taking the place of something bad in our own life as a family?

5. "Greater love has no one than this, that he lay down his life for his friends" (John 15:13). What examples of self-sacrifice did we see in the film? (For instance, when the mama bear threatens Arliss, before the dog

arrives to help, Travis puts himself between the bear and his brother. Yeller saves Travis from the javelinas and protects the family from the wolf.) Who gave His life to pay the penalty for our sins and make possible our salvation?

6. Mr. Searcy provides a negative example, always "volunteering" the help of his daughter Lisbeth without ever actually helping himself. What does Mrs. Coates think of his way of "helping"? What do you think?

Follow-Up Activities

Pop Quiz

1. In what state does the story take place?
   a) Missouri
b) Texas
c) Florida

2. Mr. Coates goes away for several months to do what?
a) rob banks
b) play a clown in a traveling circus
c) take part in a cattle drive

3. For what does Mr. Sanderson trade Old Yeller to Arliss?
a) a harmonica
b) a slingshot
c) a horned toad and a home-cooked meal

4. What's one of the symptoms of rabies in animals?
a) Uncontrollable chuckling
b) Wanting a tummy rub
c) Foaming at the mouth

Attitude Adjustment Game

Ask your child, "What were some of the hard jobs on the farm that Travis had to do in his father's absence?" Then ask, "What was his attitude as he worked?" (Usually it was pretty good, except when he was repairing damage caused by Old Yeller early in the story.) Discuss the various jobs done by the members of your family and the importance of doing what's needed even when we don't feel like it, though having a good attitude makes the work a lot more enjoyable.

Tell your kids you're going to be playing the Attitude Adjustment Game this week. Make a simple chart listing each family member's name and chores. Through the week observe how each one performs his or her chores and give a star each day for a good attitude—or no star for a bad attitude. Tell your kids they get to rate *your* attitude toward things like carpooling, cooking dinner, supervising homework, and so on. (If you have some little ones who don't have specific chores yet, assign simple tasks such as dusting, putting toys away, feeding the cat, etc.)

At the end of the week, the person with the most stars gets a special privilege or small prize. If everyone has had an equally good attitude, take the whole family to the playground, kite flying, sledding, or out for ice cream. Be sure to praise specific good attitudes and ask the kids if your household ran more smoothly and was more pleasant this week.

—Larry Weeden

The Rookie

Rated: G
Themes: Pursuing your dreams no matter what the challenge, giving support to a loved one who pursues a dream
Running Time: 2 hours, 7 minutes
Starring: Dennis Quaid as Jim Morris, Rachel Griffiths as Lori Morris, Angus T. Jones as son Hunter, Brian Cox as Jim's father, and Beth Grant as Jim's mother
Directed by: John Lee Hancock

Cautions

In the high school where Jim Morris is a teacher, a female counselor grabs his behind. (We learn soon after that she's his wife.) By the time Jim is first portrayed as an adult, his parents are divorced, with no explanation given. There are a few profanities. The players hang out in a bar and drink beer.

Story Summary

Jim Morris grew up dreaming of becoming a Major League pitcher. However, as a navy brat, he and his family moved a great deal in his childhood, making it difficult for him to stay with one team long enough to complete a season. Further, his father seemed insensitive to Jim's love of baseball and the impact of their many moves on his dream.

When the family finally settled in Big Lake, Texas, Jim discovered that the community had little interest in baseball—football was king. Making matters worse, Jim suffered a series of injuries to and operations on his pitching arm. Eventually he gave up on his dream and became a high school science teacher in Big Lake, as well as the school's baseball coach.

By the time the story takes place, he has a wife and three kids, a job, and a mortgage.

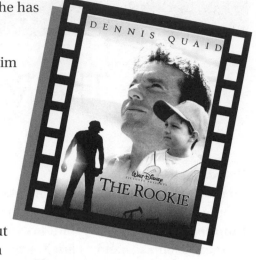

One day after practice, when Jim is 35 years old, the team's catcher encourages him to throw some pitches, and the team is greatly impressed with the coach's speed. As the team struggles to win, Jim dares them to dream, and they return the challenge. A bargain is struck: If the team wins its district championship, Jim will try out for a Major League team. With Jim throwing hard in batting practice, the team learns to hit and starts to win.

At the end of the season, the team wins district, and Jim goes to San Angelo for a tryout with the Tampa Bay Devil Rays. After waiting all day, without a warm-up, he throws 98 miles per hour—as fast as almost any major leaguer. With encouragement from his wife and son (and contrary to his dad's discouragement), Jim agrees to join the Devil Rays' minor league team in Florida.

As the season progresses, Jim misses his family greatly and agonizes over the fact that his decision means they are struggling financially. He also encounters resistance and ridicule from the other players, who think the team has accepted him only for the publicity he is generating. Nonetheless, he pitches well enough to earn promotions to the next-higher minor league and then to the Major Leagues. His first game with the Devil Rays is in Texas, against the Rangers, and most of the town of Big Lake is there to watch. Jim strikes out the only batter he faces, leading to a big post-game celebration and a reconciliation, of sorts, with his father.

A postscript tells us that Jim pitched two seasons in the Major Leagues before returning to Texas.

Before You Watch

Point out to your child that people like to give one another nicknames, especially on sports teams. Later in the movie, Jim Morris has some teammates who give him an affectionate nickname. Tell your child, "Let's keep an ear open for what that nickname is [Old Man River, or Riv] and why they call him that [because he's much older than his teammates]."

Bible Bookmarks
Ephesians 2:10; Jeremiah 29:11

Talking Points

1. Why do you think Jim Morris's father didn't support Jim's dream of becoming a Major League pitcher?

2. Why is Jim's wife reluctant at first to support his dream? What changes her mind?

3. Can anyone who wants to be a professional athlete hope to see that dream come true? Why or why not?

4. What dreams do you have at this point in your life? How can I help you to pursue them?

5. From what we saw in the movie, how does the high school team that Jim Morris coaches go from losers to winners? How do they turn their season around? (As needed, point out things like having a clear goal, growing confidence in their abilities, strong team spirit, and a leader/coach who believes in them and encourages them to pursue their dream.)

6. Why is each of these important in working to fulfill a dream? Which of these could we use more of as a family in helping you to pursue dreams at school and in your other interests?

7. After the big game, Jim gives his dad the ball. Why do you think he does that? In what way do you think it helps improve his relationship with his dad? Would you have done that? Why or why not?

Follow-Up Activities
Pop Quiz

1. In what state does most of the story take place?
a) Oklahoma
b) Arkansas
c) Texas

2. Jim Morris teaches what subject in the Big Lake high school?
a) algebra
b) science
c) English

3. Jim's dad served in which branch of the armed forces?
a) Army
b) Air Force
c) Navy

4. When he started out in the minor leagues, Jim was very discouraged and thought about quitting to go back to teaching. Why was he discouraged?
a) He missed his family and they were having a hard time paying the bills.
b) His pitching arm hurt.
c) He didn't like Florida.

5. This movie is "based on a true story." What does that mean?
a) Every word and event in the film is exactly what happened in the real-life story.
b) 50 percent of the movie is true.
c) The story stays mostly true to real life, but some scenes and dialogue are made up.

Dream Collage
Using Ephesians 2:10 ("For we are God's workmanship, created in Christ Jesus to do good works, which God prepared in advance for us to do.") plus Jeremiah 29:11 (" 'For I know the plans I have for you,' declares the LORD, 'plans to prosper you and not to harm you, plans to give you hope and a future.' "), talk about how God has exciting "dreams" for each of us, too. They may not put us in the public eye like a Major League baseball player, but they're important to God and give great purpose to our lives.

Give each family member a piece of poster board and provide markers, crayons, paints, stickers, scissors, magazines, and other art supplies. Have everyone write one of the above verses on his or her poster, with parents helping younger kids. Then, using the available art supplies, have each one (including parents) make a collage or drawing that depicts a dream they have for their future. The dream can be big or small, short-term or long-term. (Examples: win a gymnastics competition, become a teacher, dance in a ballet, learn to fly an airplane, become a missionary, compete in a spelling bee, learn to play a certain song, become an astronaut, visit another country, learn a new language, make a new friend.)

When everyone is done, have each family member present his poster and talk about his dream. Afterward, talk about how your family can support those dreams.

—Larry Weeden

Sarah, Plain & Tall

Rated: G
Themes: Family love, trust, death, fear of strangers, healing after loss
Running Time: 1 hour, 38 minutes
Starring: Glenn Close as Sarah Wheaton, Christopher Walken as Jacob Witting, Lexi Randall as Anna, Christopher Bell as Caleb, Margaret Sophie Stein as Maggie Grant, and Jon De Vries as Matthew Grant
Based on the book by Patricia MacLachlan
Directed by: Glenn Jordan

Cautions
None

Story Summary

Based on Patricia MacLachlan's Newbery Award–winning children's novel, *Sarah, Plain & Tall* was one of the most successful Hallmark Hall of Fame television specials of all time, portraying hard times on a Kansas farm in 1910.

Jacob Witting, a widowed father of two still mourning his wife's death after six long years, places an ad in the newspaper for a helper. A no-nonsense New Englander replies and agrees to come for a one-month trial visit.

Sarah Wheaton has always lived in Maine with her brother, William. Now that he's marrying, she feels she must not impose on her brother and his new wife. She's ready to see another part of the country, to do something different with her life. When her brother encourages her to stay in Maine, she says, "If I don't go now, I'll never know what it's like to have my own life."

In a letter, Jacob tells Sarah he is looking for a woman who will "make a difference," and Sarah is prepared to do just that. From the day she arrives on the Kansas farm, the children, Anna and Caleb, recognize her positive outlook and sharp confidence that has already affected them greatly through her wonderful letters. But forging a new family isn't easy. Jacob cannot let go of his grief over the death of his wife, Katherine. Anna is afraid to love Sarah because she's sure Sarah won't stay and her heart will be broken once again. Caleb is the only one who can really love Sarah wholeheartedly, for he is too young to remember his mother, and he's sure that Sarah will love them so much she'll stay. His unbounded enthusiasm concerns Jacob as he's not at all sure the arrangement will work out and result in marriage.

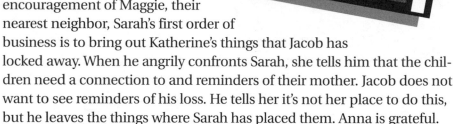

Sarah wisely does not push herself on others. Though not yet sure she will stay, she feels she must do all she can to help the family heal and move forward—to make a difference in their lives. With the encouragement of Maggie, their nearest neighbor, Sarah's first order of business is to bring out Katherine's things that Jacob has locked away. When he angrily confronts Sarah, she tells him that the children need a connection to and reminders of their mother. Jacob does not want to see reminders of his loss. He tells her it's not her place to do this, but he leaves the things where Sarah has placed them. Anna is grateful.

While Sarah is busy winning the hearts of the children and the neighbors, Jacob stubbornly clings to his grief and resists many of her ideas and efforts to help. When a storm destroys the crops and damages the house and barn, things come to a head. She tells him angrily that he doesn't need anything—there's no room in his heart for another woman.

When Maggie's baby is born, Jacob is forced to confront his grief. He finally reveals to Sarah his feelings of guilt over Katherine's death.

The next day Sarah drives the wagon to town on an errand she does not reveal to the family. Worried that she's not coming back, Anna finds that Sarah's train ticket is missing. "Go after her, Papa," Caleb chides.

Afraid that the children might be right, Jacob gallops to town. When he arrives, there is Sarah on the platform. She has turned in her ticket.

When the couple arrives home, the children tell Sarah they were afraid she left because the house is too small and she missed her old home. "I'll always miss my old home," she says. "But I'd miss you more." All is well, and the story ends with a country wedding.

Before You Watch

Life on a Kansas farm in 1910 was not like it is today. Find out about farm life during that time in history at the library. (What you find should also come in handy for understanding the Depression-era Kansas farm in *The Wizard of Oz*).

Bible Bookmarks

Matthew 25:35-40; 1 Corinthians 13, 15:21-22; Psalm 33:1-9; Genesis 29:15-30

Talking Points

1. Have you ever been the new kid on the block? When Sarah arrives in town on the train, the townspeople stare at her. How does it feel to be out of place? Do you think Jesus ever felt like an outsider? Read His story in Matthew 25:35-40. How should we treat new kids? ("Treat others as you wish to be treated.")

2. Do you know what it feels like to lose someone you love? Why do people die? (Read 1 Corinthians 15:21-22.) If someone you've loved has died, share how you felt.

3. Have you ever loved someone so much, you'd be willing to die for him or her? Why does that kind of love sometimes hurt? Parents, share with your kids how the kind of love you have for them makes you feel and why it makes you do what you do.

4. Do you think your family would have enjoyed the way life was on the Witting farm? What would have been the best parts? What would have been the worst? What convenience items available today would have made it easier? (Fast food restaurants, dishwashers, microwaves, etc.)

5. Why is singing and music so important to Caleb? Why do you think music is at the heart of worship in most churches today? Read Psalm 33:1-9 together as a family.

6. Why do you think Sarah wanted to come to Kansas? What made her stay? How is Sarah's Kansas different from Dorothy's in *The Wizard of Oz* (if you've seen that movie)?

7. Have you ever heard of "mail order brides"? Do you think they're a good idea? Why or why not? Read about how Jacob got his wife Leah in Genesis 29:15-30. Parents, if you haven't already done so, tell your kids how you met and what you liked about each other. How was your "courtship" different from Sarah and Jacob's?

Follow-Up Activities
Train Ride

Before the days of the family car and airplanes, trains were the primary mode of transportation for cross-country trips. What would it be like to have never taken a trip to a new place?

You can help your children re-create Sarah's train journey with the following activity.

Supplies
- A roll of paper, 5 to 10 inches in width (butcher paper works well)
- Construction paper
- Colored pens, pencils, or crayons
- A medium-sized cardboard box, at least 2 inches wider than the roll of paper
- Two wooden dowels or rods, 1 inch in diameter
- A box cutter
- A ruler
- Strong tape

Optional
- An electric drill
- Four short dowels or rods, 1/2 to 3/4 inch in diameter, and 4 inches in length

1) Unroll several feet of paper onto a large, flat surface. Have your children draw the scenery of the New England coast as it changes to Kansas farmland, the way it might look from a train window. Use pictures from the movie or an encyclopedia. Tell your kids that the scene

should be as long as possible and include scenes from other states that lie between Maine and Kansas. (Look in an atlas to find out what states lie between the two and what route Sarah might have taken.)

2) Turn the box upside down and cut a rectangle in the bottom, at least 2 inches from all sides, and 2 inches narrower than the roll of paper. This will be the train window. Have children use construction paper and pens to make curtains to tape to the bottom of the box.

3) Cut holes for the dowels to slide the paper across the inside of the box. Measure and use the end of a dowel to mark the width of the circles to be cut at the top and bottom on either side, at least 2 inches behind the window hole. Push the rods through.

4) When the scenery is finished, roll the paper and tape the end to the dowel inside the box. Roll it around the dowel until you come to the other end, and tape that end to the other dowel.

5) *Optional:* You can use an electric drill to drill holes in the top and bottom of the dowels and push the short dowels through the holes so the larger dowels will be held in place and make turning the scenery easier.

Your box can also be used to depict scenes from other movies as well.

Making the Sea

After Sarah takes the kids swimming, Anna tells Jacob that she had a dream about the ocean, "like glittering light on glass." Stained glass is easy to make with the many varieties of kits available at hobby or toy stores. But you can make the sea at home with blue and green crayons and wax paper. Take two sheets of wax paper and shave pieces of the crayons over one piece. When your design is done, put the other piece of wax paper over it, place a light cloth or paper towel over all layers, and use a warm (not hot) iron to melt the colors together. Cut a frame out of construction paper and glue it over the stained glass window. Trim the edges of the wax paper. Hang in a window and watch the sea colors come to life.

Just for Fun

The breed of dog that herds the sheep in the film is known as a Border collie. In the 1800s, through selective breeding by some forward-thinking shepherds, the faithful farm collie was given more desirable traits by breeding with other types of dogs—like setters for their sharp eyes and hounds for their quick and quiet natures. Today, they are considered the most useful dogs for herding sheep and livestock because of their sensitivity to commands and whistles and their ability to distinguish among them with different responses.

—*Mick Silva*

The Sound of Music

Rated: G
Themes: Faith, patience, love, courage, freedom, obedience, finding one's true vocation, the healing power of music
Running Time: 2 hours, 55 minutes
Starring: Julie Andrews as Maria, Christopher Plummer as Capt. Georg von Trapp, Eleanor Parker as Baroness Elsa Schraeder, Richard Hayden as Max Detweiler, Peggy Wood as Mother Superior, Charmian Carr as Liesl von Trapp, Heather Menzies as Louisa von Trapp, Nicholas Hammond as Freidrich von Trapp, Duane Chase as Kurt von Trapp, Angela Cartwright as Brigitta von Trapp, Debbie Turner as Marta von Trapp, Kym Karath as Gretl von Trapp, and Daniel Truhitte as Rolf Gruber
Directed by: Robert Wise

Cautions
None

Story Summary

Stern Austrian widower Capt. Georg von Trapp has difficulty keeping a suitable governess for his seven children. Meanwhile, Maria, a spirited young novice at the local convent, is struggling with her vocation. When Capt. von Trapp asks the Mother Superior for help, she thinks Maria might make a suitable governess. Reluctantly Maria obeys the abbess, leaves the convent, and takes the job.

On her first day as governess, when she sees how coldly martial the captain is with his children, Maria takes him to task. Unused to having his authority challenged, he storms out. That night at dinner, the children place a pinecone on Maria's chair as a prank. She is startled, but she keeps her cool, not telling on them, and gains points. Later, when a storm comes, Maria comforts the children by teaching them a song, "My Favorite Things." Slowly but surely, she is getting to know and love them, and they her.

Meanwhile, the captain leaves for Vienna to spend time with his love interest, Baroness Schraeder. Maria is thrilled, for now she knows why she has been sent to the von Trapp household: to prepare the children for a new mother. While the captain is away, Maria takes the children out on jaunts and teaches them to sing.

One day as they are boating on the lake bordering the captain's villa, he unexpectedly returns home—with the baroness in tow. The children are so shocked to see him, they all fall out of the boat. The captain is humiliated that his children are behaving so rowdily. When he questions Maria, she boldly tells him he has not been a proper father to his children, who desperately need him to love them. Outraged at Maria's outspokenness, the captain orders her to leave.

On her way up to her room, she stops and listens as the children sing a song she's prepared them to sing for the baroness. The captain hears the music, and his heart begins to melt. At the end of the song, he awkwardly reaches out to the children, and they respond with heartfelt hugs and tears. As Maria makes her way upstairs to gather her things, he stops her, apologizes, and thanks her for bringing music into the house once again.

Meanwhile, the children can't seem to warm up to Baroness Schraeder. She in turn is entirely unsuited to country living, having spent her life in the high society of Vienna. No fool, the baroness also notices the way the captain looks at Maria.

The baroness suggests a party, and the captain agrees to invite everyone to his villa. During the party, the captain, out for a breath of fresh air, catches Maria dancing an old Austrian folk dance. He joins her in the dance, and soon they find themselves looking deep into each other's eyes. Maria, flustered, forgets the steps. Just then the baroness appears. She suggests she and Maria talk privately.

The baroness tells Maria she's noticed how she and Georg look at each other. Maria, new at love, is genuinely confused, but she realizes that what the baroness says is true. As a young woman of principle, however, she wouldn't dream of breaking up a relationship. She decides she must return to the convent immediately, and she leaves without saying good-bye.

Back at the convent, Mother Superior calls Maria in for a talk. When she hears why Maria left, she tells her she must go back to find out if she loves the captain and he her. After all, she says, a vocation of marriage to a man is every bit as valid as a religious calling.

Maria returns, hoping to discover mutual love. The children are ecstatic. Soon, however, she hears of Georg's engagement. Devastated, she believes her questions about love and vocation have been answered. She makes plans to leave as soon as a new governess can be found to replace her.

That evening, after being confronted by the baroness about his feelings for Maria, Georg tells the baroness that their relationship is not working. She agrees, saying she's not suited to country life anyway and needs a man who's crazy about her—or at least her money. They part on friendly terms.

Georg and Maria disclose their feelings for each other and are soon married in a grand ceremony. Life is beautiful: The couple couldn't be happier, the children are thrilled with their new mother, and their friend Max has persuaded the family to sing at the upcoming Salzburg Folk Festival.

Alas, the times are out of joint. Georg receives orders to report for active service in the navy of Nazi Germany. A man of principle and an Austrian to the core, he doesn't see how he can obey these orders. The family makes plans to escape Austria.

Fun-loving, apolitical Max agrees to abet the refugees. He helps them concoct a plan to flee during the Folk Festival. Each member will disappear offstage after an elaborate exit routine, meet up with the others, and escape by car over the border. When the Nazis give chase, the family heads toward the convent where the sisters hide them in their graveyard. Liesl gasps when she sees Rolf, her boyfriend turned

Nazi, and a tense moment ensues as the captain deals with the young man. But with a little help from the sisters, the family escapes over the Alps to freedom.

 ## Before You Watch

The great-grandchildren of the real Capt. von Trapp live in Montana and perform around the United States. Check www.vontrappchildren.com or www.trappfamily.com for dates and venues. If they're coming to a town near you, it would be fun to take your family to see them. If not, you can read about the family on the Web sites before watching the movie.

Bible Bookmarks

Romans 13:1-7; Exodus 23:2; Acts 5:29

Talking Points

1. What do you think about Maria and her faith? Is it genuine or just part of her culture? What are some of the ways Maria expresses her faith in the convent?

2. When is it right to obey authority? Is it ever right to disobey? What are some of the times in the movie when characters disobeyed authority? What does the Bible say about authorities (Romans 13:1-7)? What does the Bible say about wrongdoing (Exodus 23:2)?

3. After his first wife dies, Captain von Trapp banishes all music from the house. Why do you think he does this? Can this ever be a good thing?

4. When the von Trapp family is escaping from the Nazis, the sisters hide them in the convent. Can you think of anywhere in the Bible where people were hidden from authorities? (David in 1 Samuel, the Hebrew spies in Joshua)

5. Do you think the sisters would have been in trouble if the Nazis had caught the von Trapps? At the end of this scene the sisters do something to thwart the Nazis. What is it? Is it a right or wrong thing to do? Why? (See Acts 5:29.)

Follow-Up Activities

Nazi Invasion Game

This game is a variation on "Red Light, Green Light." It is best played in a park or large grassy area. The object is to escape from the Nazis. A parent acts as the Secret Service, standing with his or her back turned toward the starting line, while everyone else is a von Trapp child attempting to make it to the safety line 30 feet away without being "caught." The SS cannot chase them, but can only "catch" the children if he sees them moving when he turns around. If a child is spotted, he is "frozen" and must remain where he is. Children can "free" their siblings if they touch them while the SS isn't looking. The game is over when the children make it to the safety line or when all have been captured.

After the game, talk about how the von Trapps and people fleeing the Nazis at this time in Austria must have felt (scared, hopeless, angry, and so on). Discuss how God gives us courage and hope through the Bible's promises such as Proverbs 28:1 and Psalm 31:24.

True Heroes

(This activity is for older kids who are able to handle the details of the Holocaust.) Like the sisters, many ordinary people had to make hard decisions about whether to obey the Nazi authorities or possibly lose their lives for disobeying. Corrie ten Boom's family went to the concentration camps for hiding Jews. Dietrich Bonhoeffer was a German Christian who stood up to the Nazis at the cost of his life. Over several nights, read *The Hiding Place* by Corrie ten Boom or listen with your family to *Bonhoeffer: The Cost of Freedom* (Focus on the Family Radio Theatre). Talk about the hard choices these Christians had to make. How did their faith in God help them choose what to do?

—*Jan P. Dennis*

Spy Kids

Rated: PG
Themes: Secrets, sibling rivalry, working together, family values, courage, unity, valuing the gifts of others
Running Time: 1 hour, 28 minutes
Starring: Antonio Banderas as Gregorio Cortez, Carla Gugino as Ingrid Cortez, Alexa Vega as Carmen Cortez, Daryl Sabara as Juni Cortez, Alan Cumming as Fegan Floop, Tony Shalhoub as Alexander Minion, Teri Hatcher as Ms. Gradenko, Robert Patrick as Mr. Lisp, Cheech Marin as Felix Gumm, Danny Trejo as Machete, and a brief cameo by George Clooney as Devlin
Directed by: Robert Rodriguez

Cautions

There are verbal put-downs between siblings. Carmen, in an upsetting situation says, "Shii—take mushrooms." It sounds as though she is about to say something else. There are many scenes of people getting bonked or thrown—but there are no serious injuries or blood. The many cool gadgets make the film less frightening.

Story Summary

Carmen and Juni Cortez are sister and brother in a very normal family—or are they? So many secrets in the Cortez family keep everyone from knowing who each other really is. The biggest secret is that the parents, Ingrid and Gregorio Cortez, are former international spies. Now that important OSS agents have disappeared, Gregorio is called back into service to help find and rescue them. Ingrid wants to join the adventure and save the world again. So, off they go, leaving their children in the capable hands of another spy masquerading as "Uncle" Felix.

Meanwhile, a children's television show host, a man named Floop, is asked by an evil man, Mr. Lisp, to develop an army he can use to take over the world. Floop tries to create an army by mutating the captured OSS agents into characters for his TV show and calling them Fooglies. But that idea fizzles when, during the mutating process, the agents' brains turn to mush.

So Floop tries again—making robot children who look identical to real children of dignitaries throughout the world. He calls them Spy Kids, and, once pro-grammed, they are unstoppable. The only problem with them is that their brains don't work either. They can only mutter unintelligible elec-tronic noises, giving away the fact that they aren't real children, but robots.

Floop and his sidekick, Minion, are determined to retrieve a small intelligence device called The Third Brain, which Gregorio Cortez helped the OSS develop back when he was a spy.

Ingrid and Gregorio are kidnapped by Floop. This situation causes "Uncle" Felix to divulge to Carmen and Juni his real identity and the identity of the children's parents. Carmen says, "My parents aren't cool enough to be spies." Felix urges the children into a high-tech shuttle, which is programmed to take them to a safe house. The safe house is filled with spy gadgets, including The Third Brain, and instructions on how to be a spy. The children are immersing themselves in their new world of spying when agents burst in and take The Third Brain.

From this point on, the story is a junior James Bond thriller complete with lots of gadgets and chase scenes, close calls, failures, and successes.

Carmen and Juni bicker and quarrel, like most siblings, through much of the film, mostly with Carmen putting Juni down. Their quarrel-ing gets them into trouble more than once, until they discover they need to work together if they are going to succeed in saving their parents.

The children enlist the help of Gregorio's brother Machete—a

118

counterintelligence equipment designer. He refuses to help, but he serves them dinner and shows them a device that can take them to Floop's castle.

Floop truly has no interest in building an army. What he really wants is to build a great kids' TV show. We find out that Minion is the true force behind all the diabolical schemes.

The children arrive at the castle, then must begin the process of rescuing their parents. In the end, it's the children who utilize their unique skills, working together and encouraging each other to be successful.

Before You Watch
You may need to explain what a spy is to your younger children. You might even tell your kids that spies are used by America to help protect our country.

Bible Bookmarks
Ecclesiastes 4:12; Matthew 5:22

Talking Points
1. Have you ever stopped believing what someone says because they've either lied or kept secrets that shouldn't have been kept? How did it feel to not be able to trust that person? Can you count how many secrets the Cortez family keep from each other? Don't forget the secrets Juni and Carmen speak of when they are in the safe house. Are there any secrets you should share with your family now?

2. Do you think your parents are cool or uncool? What do you think they could do to make themselves cool? Do you think they've always been uncool? Ask them to tell you a story about something cool they used to do before they had you.

3. Find out what the word *sacrifice* means. What do your parents sacrifice to make the family fun more important than their own fun?

4. Talk about the names Carmen calls Juni. How do you think Juni feels? Have you ever called your brother or sister names? How did you feel when you were saying those things? How do you think they felt? Ask him or her right now to see if you were right.

5. When do Carmen and Juni really start accomplishing things that will help their parents? What do you do to help the family work together toward common goals? What do you do that keeps that from happening?

6. Talk about the importance of family. What makes a family important to each other? What can a family do for each other that others can't do? Some families go to the park together, others throw a ball back and forth. Some talk about movies. Some talk about God and their relationship with Him. What does your family talk about that shows that you are different from other families?

7. What does the Bible say about doing things alone? Read Ecclesiastes 4:12: "Though one may be overpowered, two can defend themselves. A cord of three strands is not quickly broken." Can you think of ways you can help your family be stronger?

Follow-Up Activities

Missing Ingredient

Give each family member an ingredient to bake cookies. (Make sure your ingredient is sugar.) Tell your kids you have decided to leave the sugar out and ask them if that's okay with them. Ask how they think the cookies will taste without the sugar. After everyone's had a chance to share his or her opinion, mix up the cookies, leaving out the sugar. Then mix up another batch of cookies *with* sugar. When the cookies are done, have everyone try both kinds. Ask what's wrong with the sugarless cookies. Talk about how important it is to work together as a family and how when one person doesn't contribute, things don't turn out as well—like cookies without sugar.

Learning to Share

Give one person a stack of paper to paint on, and give everyone paints. Ask your kids what will happen if that family member doesn't share the paper. What will happen if he or she does share? Pass out the paper and ask everyone to paint a picture about different ways families work together.

Name-Calling

Do your kids call each other hurtful names? This week, set up a jar in a prominent place. Read Matthew 5:22. Tell the kids that each time someone hears a family member calling a sibling a name, the name-caller must put 25 cents into the jar. At the end of the week see how much money you have collected and talk about how you might reduce that amount the next week. If at the end of the next week the amount is less, celebrate. Continue to use the jar until name-calling is rare. If the name-calling doesn't go away, increase the amount to 50 cents, then a dollar, and so on until name-calling is not worth the high price.

—*Lissa Halls Johnson*

Stuart Little 2

Rated: G
Themes: Courage, friendship, importance of family, love, embracing differences, second chances, honesty, forgiveness
Running Time: 1 hour, 15 minutes
Starring: The voices of Michael J. Fox as Stuart Little, Melanie Griffith as Margalo, Nathan Lane as Snowbell, and James Woods as Falcon; and with actors Geena Davis as Mrs. Little, Hugh Laurie as Mr. Little, and Jonathon Libnicki as George Little
Based on the book by E. B. White
Directed by: Rob Minkoff

Cautions

There is mild language and name-calling. Snowbell says, "I'm going to be Falcon poop." Falcon may be intimidating for younger viewers. Despite intense circumstances, Snowbell's wackiness diffuses most of the fear. George and Stuart both ask each other to "cover" for them by lying to their parents.

Story Summary

Stuart is back. The small mouse with a big heart returns for a new adventure. Stuart has settled into his place in the Little family, complete with new addition Baby Martha. But George is getting older and making other friends. Stuart feels a little lonely and wishes for a friend of his own. When Stuart accidentally wrecks the model airplane that he and George have been building together, he causes his already overprotective mother to be more cautious and George to be upset. Dad comes to the rescue and encourages Stuart by saying, "Every cloud has a silver lining."

Stuart's silver lining arrives in the form of a tiny bird named Margalo. Stuart is thrilled to have found a friend just his size. He rescues Margalo from the evil Falcon and their friendship is sealed. Stuart takes Margalo home to care for her injured wing, not realizing Margalo is a con working for Falcon. She tricks Stuart into believing that she's hurt and then plans to steal from the Littles. But the love and compassion that she sees in the Little family causes her to question her agenda. She doesn't want to hurt the Littles and she definitely doesn't want to hurt her new friend. Falcon gives her no choice. She steals Mrs. Little's ring and disappears from Stuart's life.

Stuart feels certain that Falcon has captured Margalo and is holding her prisoner. He (along with Snowbell) embarks on a mission to rescue his friend. Unfortunately he asks George to cover for his absence by lying to their parents. George convinces their parents that Stuart is constantly away rehearsing for the school play. The lies continue when George recruits his friend Will to lie for him. Will lies for George but says, "If I was smart, I wouldn't be in this situation."

Meanwhile Stuart finds Falcon and realizes the truth. Margalo assures him that she's sincerely sorry and never meant to hurt him. Stuart forgives her, but now they must escape from Falcon.

George becomes tangled up in all the lies and starts to feel stressed. As with most lies, the truth eventually comes out. Mr. and Mrs. Little sit down with George and address the issue of lying. George tells his parents where Stuart went and the family goes to rescue him. Stuart goes up against Falcon and wins. Falcon tries to intimidate Margalo, but she returns the ring anyway and is forgiven by Mrs. Little. Her friendship is renewed with the Littles. And Stuart has proven his character by never giving up on Margalo.

Before You Watch

Kids will enjoy *Stuart Little 2* more if they are already familiar with the story of Stuart Little. If your kids haven't seen the first Stuart Little movie, watch it, or better yet, read E. B. White's original children's book together before your movie night. Also, the Little family enjoys eating marshmallows together—maybe your family can do the same.

Bible Bookmarks

Exodus 20:16; Colossians 3:9; Matthew 5:37; Titus 1:2; John 8:32; 1 Samuel 16:7; Philippians 4:13

Talking Points

1. Close to the beginning of the film George asks Stuart to tell Mom and Dad that he walked him home, even though he didn't. Stuart also asks George to lie for him when he goes to find Margalo. Are these good reasons for lying? What are some other reasons to lie? Once you begin to lie, like George finds out, it's hard to stop. Read what the Bible has to say about lying in Exodus 20:16, Colossians 3:9, and Matthew 5:37. Does God lie? (Read Titus 1:2.) Think of a few different scenarios when it would seem easy to lie. What would you do in each circumstance? (Examples: when you don't want to do something, when you're scared, or when you're trying to impress someone.)

2. Stuart doesn't let the fact that he's smaller than everyone else hinder his ability to enjoy life. All children are different, and respecting differences is important. It is never okay to make fun of people who are different. Margalo and Stuart become close friends even though they are very different. Do you have friends who look or act different? What qualities do you appreciate in your friends? Remember that God never judges you by the way you look. Read 1 Samuel 16:7.

3. Talk about the control that Falcon holds over Margalo. When Margalo stands up to Falcon, she says that she is "free." Can sin have a hold over us? What happens when we obey God and confess our sins? Read John 8:32. Are you "free"?

4. Margalo tells Stuart that "you are as big as you feel." What does that mean? Have you ever felt intimidated by someone bigger or stronger than you? What did you do? Remember you can be confident

that God is always with you and He helps you do great things. Read Philippians 4:13.

5. Mrs. Little is very protective of Stuart. Why do you think that is? Like Mrs. Little, your parents are protective of you because they love you very much and want you to be safe and healthy. Parents, talk about what it means to protect a family from both physical and spiritual harm and why you have some of the family rules you do.

Follow-Up Activities

Break the Lies!

Little sins add up to big sins, and breaking away from a pattern of sin isn't easy. Give each family member a piece of paper. Ask if they can easily tear their pieces in half. Once everyone attempts to tear the paper, hand them a few more sheets. This time have your kids write on their sheets of paper sins such as "stealing" or "lying." Now have them try to tear their stacks of paper. Repeat this until no one is able to tear through their "sins."

Ask your kids these questions: Have you ever been able to break a habit of sin? What happened? What happens when you don't break the habit and you keep doing it? Why do you think that is?

Read James 1:12-15 and talk about ways to avoid sin and the importance of forgiveness when we do sin. If you're comfortable, talk about breaking out of sins that you've found yourself trapped in (being sure it's appropriate for kids). Remind your kids that they can always come to you for help with this.*

Family Greeting

How do people of other cultures and nationalities greet each other? (For example: In Japan, families often bow; Australians greet each other with "G'day, mate!" In the New Testament, Paul often begins his letters with "Grace and peace to you in Christ Jesus.") The Littles have a special way of greeting each other. What is it? Have everyone in the family come up with a few ideas for a special saying or movement you might share as a family and then practice greeting each other in the new way.

Just for Fun

E. B. White said he wrote *Stuart Little* after having a dream one night of a little boy who acted like a mouse. White is also the author of *Charlotte's Web* and *Trumpet of the Swan*, two books that have also been transformed into fun-filled animated films.

—*Brandy Bruce*

* Adapted from *Simple Science Family Nights Tool Chest,* by Jim Weidmann and Mark DeNooy, with Kurt Bruner. Colorado Springs: Cook Communications, 1999, p. 63.

Swiss Family Robinson (1960)

Rated: G
Themes: Respect, ingenuity, pride, covetousness, jealousy, family, faith, stereotypes, gender roles, loyalty
Running Time: 2 hours, 6 minutes
Starring: Sir John Mills as Father Robinson, Dorothy McGuire as Mother Robinson, James MacArthur as Fritz, Janet Munro as Roberta, Tommy Kirk as Ernst, Kevin Corcoran as Francis, and Sessue Hayakawa as Kuala
Based on the book by Johann David Wyss
Directed by: Ken Annakin

Cautions

This exciting representation of Johann David Wyss's classic adventure story (based on *Robinson Crusoe*) of a family learning to survive on a deserted tropical island is unapologetically family-friendly. No foul language or sexuality mars this film. And the complete lack of authenticity lends a comfortable (sometimes comical) distance to the slapstick peril and violence. Run-ins with gila monsters, tigers, sharks, and a giant water snake convey a "PBS Nature Special" feel. At one point, the older brothers' jealousy over Roberta escalates into a short fistfight. The intensity of the final pirate battle is conveyed with suspense-building music rather than gore. Stereotypical bad guys die bloodlessly from guns, arrows, and coconut bombs; fall from cliffs, and into various booby traps, including a tiger pit; fight each other with swords; and tumble down hills as boulders and logs topple them.

Story Summary

After miraculously surviving a storm at sea, the ship-wrecked Robinsons must build a makeshift raft and paddle to an uncharted desert isle. Over the coming months they will build a house in a giant tree and learn to survive harsh storms, wild beasts, and the constant threat of pirate attacks. Through bravery, cooperation, and creativity, the father must lead his family in building shelter and safeguarding his remaining possession of value—a God-honoring family—from the wild.

When the older boys, Fritz and Ernst, are allowed to set out to explore the rest of the island, they happen upon a sea captain and his grandson being held captive by the cutthroat pirates. The boys bravely rescue the grandson, but they barely escape before the pirates discover them. As they make their way back, "grandson" Bertie is revealed to be Roberta, the sole single girl on the island. This sets up some inevitable competition between the brothers who vie for her attention.

They return to the tree house, but with the pirates' hostage now in their possession, they must prepare a defense. The pirates will soon find them, and the industrious family is forced to devise several defensive plans to protect themselves. When the pirates do attack, the Robinsons courageously stand together to defend against the onslaught, but they are inevitably overwhelmed. As all appears lost, Roberta's grandfather's fleet arrives in the nick of time to send the scurvy barbarians fleeing to safety.

Now that they have been rescued, the Robinsons realize how happy they've been on the island. They have a choice to make: Go on to New Guinea, return to Europe, or stay on the island and start a new colony. All but Ernst decide to stay. Grateful that the boys rescued Roberta, her grandfather has offered to send Ernst to college. But not surprisingly, Roberta decides to stay and marry Fritz.

Before You Watch

This movie is based on a classic book, which has many modernized versions. To find an appropriate version to read before your movie night, check out a couple from your library and look through them for suitability. While the original novel itself is long and somewhat tedious to get through, some of the other treatments of the tale are more palatable for younger children.

Bible Bookmarks

Genesis 1:26-31; Matthew 25:14-30; Genesis 11:1-9; Genesis 25:21-34; Proverbs 3:13-20

Talking Points

1. How would you feel about having your own island? Do you think you'd miss your friends? School? Candy? What other things would you have to do without? Would you be able to do it? Have you ever gone without those things for a long time? What was it like?

2. Do you think Francis should have been punished for disobeying his mother and trapping the baby elephant? Do you think he learns his lesson? What does he do when he is told to leave the coconut bombs alone? If you were Francis's parent, what would you do to make him obey?

3. What are some of the animals the family learns to use as helpers? (A sea turtle, an elephant, a donkey, a tiger.) What are some of the other animals on the island? Why do you think God made so many different types of animals? Which are your favorites?

4. In the movie, what are some of the different uses for these things: coconuts, palm leaves, logs, vines? When someone is good at making use of the things he has available, people say he is "industrious." Jesus told a story about three servants who had different levels of industriousness in Matthew 25:14-30. Read that together in a children's Bible and talk about what it means to be industrious.

5. The pirates are supposed to be of Asian descent, while the Robinsons are Swiss. What does *descent* mean? Where did different cultures, races, and languages come from? Read Genesis 11:1-9. Why did God scatter the people?

6. Fritz and Ernst are very competitive, especially over Roberta. If you have a brother or a sister (or a friend), do you fight or do you get along most of the time? Are you similar or different? Would you prefer to fight or would you rather get along? Jacob and Esau didn't get along very well, even before they were born! Read about them in Genesis 25:21-34.

7. When the family is rescued by the captain, why do they decide to stay? What would you have done: stayed or gone? Why is Ernst so eager to leave for school? Do you like school? Are there some parts you like better than others? Just like life, sometimes there are things in school we don't like. What does the Bible say you should do when you don't like something? Read Proverbs 3:13-20.

Follow-Up Activities

Swiss Family Survivor

Next time you go camping, play "Swiss Family Robinson." You can fight off pirates by fashioning booby traps out of rope and sticks, making a log tumbler, and devising pinecone "coconut bombs." Be as elaborate or as simple as you like with what you have available. If you aren't going camping anytime soon, you can do the same thing in your backyard. Your family might even want to build a tree house.

Industriousness Game

Imagine you are all stranded on a desert island with no electricity, running water, or modern devices. Provide paper and pencils (graph paper and colored pencils are especially fun for this exercise). Have each family member draw a diagram for a contraption or a plan that illustrates how they would solve one of the following problems using only the things the Robinsons had available in the movie. The plans must be specific and offer proof that the contraption or solution would work. After everyone presents their plans, give certificates for the most creative plan, most inventive plan, most practical plan, and so on.

1. Move a big boulder.
2. Make a soft bed.
3. Catch a bird.
4. Cut your hair.
5. Keep bugs out of your food.
6. Celebrate a birthday with special food and decorations.

Just for Fun

Did your family notice that the animals that live on the island would never exist together in one place—unless the place were a zoo? Some are native to Asia, some to Africa, and the rest to other parts of the world. See if your family can name where the various animals would come from. Remember that Asian elephants have small ears while African elephants have large ears. Which type lives on the island? (Asian)

—*Mick Silva*

Tarzan (1999)

Rated: G
Themes: The importance of family, accepting those who are different, obeying parents, fear, courage, maturity, God's protection, orphans, pleasing God, having Jesus "in your heart"
Running Time: 1 hour, 28 minutes
Starring: The voices of Tony Goldwyn as Tarzan, Minnie Driver as Jane, Rosie O'Donnell as Terk, Glenn Close as Kala, Lance Henriksen as Kerchak, Brian Blessed as Clayton, Wayne Knight as Tantor, Nigel Hawthorne as Professor Porter, and Alex D. Linz as Young Tarzan
Directed by: Chris Buck and Kevin Lima

Cautions

In true Disney tradition, baby Tarzan's parents are killed by a leopard—but the incident occurs offscreen. Other intense moments include a villain accidentally hanging himself—also out of frame. The sexuality is low-voltage: The puzzled Tarzan lifts the hem of Jane's dress and later puts his ear to her chest, listening for her heartbeat. Language is inoffensive, except when an elephant exclaims, "My butt!" Professor Porter also says, "Good Lord!"

Story Summary

In this version of the Edgar Rice Burroughs classic, it's all about family. The action-packed opening sequence depicts the shipwreck of a mother, father, and infant on the African coast. The parents immediately set up housekeeping, Swiss Family Robinson–style, in an elaborate tree house. But tragedy strikes when Sabor, a leopard, attacks.

A female gorilla named Kala, who lost her own baby to the leopard, discovers a trail of blood-red paw prints in the tree house. Mom and Dad have perished, but the baby has survived. Sabor tries to finish the job, but the protective Kala saves the child—and names him Tarzan.

Kala is happy to mother the little human, but her mate, Kerchak—the gruff leader of the pack—doesn't want to play daddy. "He will never be one of us," Kerchak growls. Fortunately, Tarzan's adoptive cousin, Terk, isn't so prejudiced against *homo sapiens*—unlike other young gorillas in the community.

Longing to win the blessing of his new "father," Tarzan vows to "be the best ape ever." He grows up, learning the ways of the jungle as he plays with friends Terk and Tantor, an elephant prone to panic attacks. As a young adult, Tarzan gets a chance to prove himself when the vicious Sabor tries to kill Kerchak. Tarzan slays the leopard, but still, Kerchak fails to welcome the apeman into the family.

Tarzan's world is upended as gunshots herald the arrival of more humans—the gorilla-studying Professor Porter; his daughter, Jane; and rifle-wielding Clayton, who purports to protect the Porters but has more nefarious plans. Scoffing at the Porters' claim that the gorillas have "family groups," Clayton thinks apes are beasts best shot, stuffed, or sold. He feels the same way about Tarzan, even after the latter rescues Jane from a horde of baboons.

The apeman, pressing his palm to Jane's, discovers they're the same "kind." Jane and her father undertake an intense English as a Second Language program with the jungle man, and soon he's saying, "Me Tarzan, you Jane"—though, inexplicably, without the British accents of his tutors.

Jane's charms overwhelm Tarzan, who wants to bring her home to meet his simian parents. The Porters and Clayton nag him to do just that, wanting to find the apes for their own reasons. But Kerchak warns Tarzan to protect the gorillas by keeping the humans away.

When the boat arrives to bring the Britons back to civilization, Tarzan finally agrees to show them where the apes live—hoping Jane will stay. The meeting is peaceful until Kerchak decides to defend his species, leading to a fight with Tarzan. Defeated, Kerchak says, "I asked you to protect our family . . . and you betrayed us all."

Confused by conflicting loyalties, Tarzan is brought by Kala to a place he doesn't remember—the tree house his birth parents built. Amid the ruins he finds a family portrait and discovers who he really is. "I just want you to be happy," says Kala, "whatever you decide."

Tarzan chooses to go with the other humans on the boat. "No matter where I go, you will always be my mother," he tells Kala.

"And you will always be in my heart," she replies.

Danger lurks on the ship, however, where Clayton and his men imprison Tarzan in the hold with Jane and her father. Clayton's scheme: to capture and sell the gorillas.

Tantor and Terk swim to the ship and free Tarzan, who tries to alert the apes. But Clayton's forces are already trapping the gorillas. Clayton is about to shoot Kerchak when Tarzan arrives and liberates the "father" who has always rejected him.

"You came back," Kerchak says in wonder.

"I came home," the apeman replies.

The battle with Clayton reaches a fever pitch. When he accidentally hangs himself on a vine, it's over.

Mortally wounded, Kerchak tells Tarzan, "Forgive me for not understanding that you have always been one of us." Asking the apeman to be the new protector of the tribe, he finally calls Tarzan his son.

It's time for Jane and the professor to leave. They take a dinghy to the ship, but halfway there, they realize their hearts are with the apeman and his apes. They swim back to the jungle, leaving the ship's captain to explain their absence to polite society.

Before You Watch

If you're renting this movie, look through the store with your child to see how many other versions of the Tarzan story you can find. There are dozens, including the silent picture *Tarzan of the Apes* with Elmo Lincoln (1918); *Tarzan the Ape Man* with Johnny Weissmuller (1932); *Greystoke: The Legend of Tarzan, Lord of the Apes* with Christopher

Lambert (1984); and *Tarzan and Jane* (2002), a not-so-successful "sequel" to this animated feature that combined three episodes of a Disney cartoon series. And don't forget *George of the Jungle* with Brendan Fraser (1997), a live-action spoof that scored a hit in theaters.

Explain that apes play a big role in *Tarzan*. If you live near a zoo, visit the gorillas, note their behavior, and be ready to compare it with those of the animals in the movie. If you don't live near a zoo, check out a library book (or back issue of *National Geographic*) that describes these fascinating creatures God has made, and the ways in which they relate to each other.

Bible Bookmarks

Jeremiah 49:11; James 1:27; Romans 15:7; Exodus 20:12, Psalm 103:8-14; Genesis 1:18-24; Colossians 3:20; Matthew 26:2; 2 Timothy 1:7

Talking Points

1. Which did you think was scariest: (a) the shipwreck, (b) Tarzan's loss of his parents, (c) the leopard's efforts to get baby Tarzan, or (d) the battle with Clayton at the end? Why? When you feel scared, what do you do? Read Psalm 32:7. How could remembering this verse help?

2. Which characters in this movie act as protectors? Who are some people who protect you? Why do they do it? What's one way in which you could thank one of your protectors this week?

3. Who is an orphan in this movie, and who steps in to take care of him? How do you think God feels about orphans? Read Jeremiah 49:11 and James 1:27 to find out.

4. Who has a hard time accepting young Tarzan? Why is it hard to accept those who are different from us in some way? Read Romans 15:7. Who might God want you to work on accepting this week?

5. Why does Tarzan try so hard to please Kerchak? Do you think most kids try that hard to please their parents? Should they? Is Tarzan just following the idea behind Exodus 20:12, or is something else going on? Explain.

6. This movie's most popular song is "You'll Be in My Heart." When Kala tells Tarzan he'll always be in her heart even if he goes away, what

does she mean? When people say they have Jesus "in their hearts," what do they mean?

7. Kerchak warns Tarzan to keep the other humans away in order to protect the gorillas, but Tarzan disobeys. What do you think he should have done? Why? When was the last time you had to choose whether to obey your parents (see Colossians 3:20)? What did you do?

Follow-Up Activities
Tarzan Yell

If your child is young, head for a playground and clamber around on a jungle gym. Stage a "Tarzan Yell" contest. Then talk about Bible characters who were outdoor adventurers—like David, Esau, and Moses.

Sibling Unity

Tarzan affirms the idea of accepting every member of the family. Are sibling rivalry, personality differences, adoption, or the blending of two families making acceptance a challenge in your home? Hand your children paper and pencil and ask them to list the things they have in common—anything from last year's vacation to freckles to a fondness for macaroni and cheese. Award a small prize to the person who names the most similarities. Encourage your kids to concentrate on these, rather than differences, during the coming week.

Just for Fun

Take a close look at the scene in which Tantor and the gorillas discover the humans' camp. Several "frightening" man-made items, alien to the animals, are shown. One is a teapot. Does it look familiar? If you've seen *Beauty and the Beast*, another animated Disney feature, it should. Note the remarkable resemblance to the teapot in that movie, a talking version voiced by Angela Lansbury.

—*John Duckworth*

Toy Story 2

Rated: G
Themes: Materialism, sharing, importance of relationships, the need to be loved, lasting treasures, self-sacrifice, greed, forgiveness, valuing those devalued by others
Running Time: 1 hour, 35 minutes
Starring: The voices of Tom Hanks as Woody, Tim Allen as Buzz Lightyear, Joan Cusack as Jessie, Kelsey Grammer as the Prospector, Don Rickles as Mr. Potato Head, Wallace Shawn as Rex, John Ratzenberger as Hamm, Jim Varney as Slinky Dog, Wayne Knight as Al, Annie Potts as Bo Peep, Jodi Benson as Barbie, Joe Ranft as Wheezy and John Morris as Andy
Directed by: John Lasseter, Lee Unkrich, and Ash Brannon

Cautions

You'll hear plenty of arguing among the characters, but no profanity. Several moments of suspense are intense, but shouldn't disturb any but the youngest and most sensitive children. Be warned, though, that the DVD's unrated special-feature "outtakes" include a flatulent Prospector demonstrating why he's called Stinky Pete and playing "dirty old man" in a conversation with twin Barbies. The latter may not register with younger children, but could offend parents.

Story Summary

Woody, Buzz Lightyear, and the other plucky playthings from *Toy Story* return in a sequel that's just as entertaining—and more thought-provoking—than the original.

Andy, the toys' owner, is about to leave for cowboy camp when he accidentally rips Woody's arm. Andy decides to leave Woody behind, a depressing development for the miniature buckaroo.

"Toys don't last forever," says Andy's mom, who proceeds to set up a yard sale in front of the house. Wheezy the Penguin, suffering from a broken squeaker, finds himself in the 25-cent box. Woody tries to rescue him but is kidnapped by Al McWhiggin, a greedy toy collector who runs Al's Toy Barn (and does his own TV commercials in a chicken suit).

Al has a plan: to make big bucks by refurbishing Woody and selling him to a Japanese toy museum, along with other toys from a classic TV series called *Woody's Roundup.* Imprisoned in Al's apartment, Woody learns his true identity as a showbiz star from his fellow collectibles—Jessie the Yodeling Cowgirl, Stinky Pete the Prospector, and Bullseye the Horse. Jessie and Stinky Pete, sick of being shut up in dark boxes, are eager to go to the museum. Woody is their ticket out, since the buyer wants only a complete set. Woody, however, wants to return to Andy.

That's what Buzz Lightyear and Woody's other friends want, too. They undertake a mission to rescue Woody from Al's greasy clutches.

After being cleaned and stitched, Woody spots a vent through which to escape. Jessie is beside herself, dreading the limbo of storage. She bitterly recalls the girl who outgrew and abandoned her and warns that the same thing will happen to Woody. The Prospector points out that Andy is growing up and will lose interest in his toys. "You can stay with us and last forever," he tells Woody. "You'll be adored by children for generations."

Not wanting to let his new friends down, Woody decides to stick with them. "Who am I to break up the *Roundup* gang?" he asks.

Buzz, meanwhile, is trapped in a package on the shelf in Al's store— and replaced by a clueless clone who leads the toys in a search for his nemesis, Zurg. By the time they're rejoined by the real Buzz, they've broken into Woody's prison.

When Woody explains that he doesn't want to go, Buzz reminds him, "Life's only worth living if you're being loved by a kid."

"This is my only chance!" Woody protests.

"To do what, Woody?" Buzz asks. "Watch kids from behind glass and never be loved again? Some life." Disappointed, Buzz and friends leave.

Watching a clip from his old TV show, Woody sees himself say, "The real treasures are your friends and family." Scraping the paint off the bottom of his shoe, he rediscovers the name ANDY. Woody realizes that his owner will grow up, but he doesn't want to miss the time they still have together. Deciding to leave with Buzz and the gang, he invites his *Roundup* pals to come along.

The Prospector, however, isn't interested. He tightens the vent screws with his pickax, ensuring the toys will be sent to the museum. Al arrives and hauls them to the airport.

After another run-in with Zurg, Buzz and friends pursue Woody in a pizza delivery truck. A nick-of-time rescue on the runway keeps the *Roundup* cast from being shanghaied to Japan—though the devious Stinky Pete ends up in the hands of a girl who likes to give her toys radical makeovers.

The toys return home, joined by Jessie and Bullseye. Andy fixes Woody, who says that someday, when the boy doesn't want to play anymore, "I'll have Buzz Lightyear to keep me company—for infinity and beyond."

Before You Watch

Toy Story 2 stands on its own. But if you and your child haven't seen the original *Toy Story*, consider viewing it together first. Getting acquainted with the characters and their relationships, especially the contentious bond between Woody and Buzz, will help you appreciate the latter's rescue mission—and the former's pledge of friendship "for infinity and beyond."

Take a field trip to a toy store and see how many classic toys (Mr. Potato Head, Slinky Dog, Etch-a-Sketch, Barbie, plastic army men, a piggy bank, etc.) you can find. When it's time to watch the movie, your child will have fun recognizing these Baby Boomer favorites.

Bible Bookmarks

Matthew 6:19-21, 25:31-40; 1 John 1:9, 4:16-19; John 15:13; Luke 12:15-21; Hebrews 13:5

Talking Points

1. When Andy leaves Woody behind, Woody dreams that Andy says, "You're broken. I don't want to play with you anymore." How do most kids tend to treat others who have something "wrong" with them? Read Matthew 25:31-40. How do you think God wants us to treat people who are "broken"?

2. Wheezy the Penguin, put on the shelf because his squeaker doesn't work, says, "We're all just one stitch away" from being sold in a yard sale. What do you think he means? Is this how God feels about us, always ready to punish us or throw us away if we don't please Him? Read 1 John 1:9 and 1 John 4:16-19 to find out.

3. Buzz says, "Woody once risked his life to save me. I couldn't call myself his friend if I weren't willing to do the same." How is this like Jesus' saying in John 15:13? How did Jesus prove His friendship with us?

4. Al's apartment, where he keeps his most valuable toys, has a sign on it saying, "No Children Allowed." Why? Do you have any toys you don't want other kids to play with? Why? When it comes to sharing, how are you like Al? How are you different?

5. If Woody and the *Roundup* gang had ended up in the toy museum, do you think they would have been happy? Explain. Do you think it's better to be admired by others from a distance, or to be their friends? Why?

6. Woody says on the old TV show, "The real treasures are your friends and family." What do you think he means? Read Matthew 6:19-21. What do you think Jesus means?

7. When Al does that last commercial in his chicken suit, why is he crying? If things had turned out differently and he'd sold Woody and the other toys, do you think he would have been happy? For how long? Read Jesus' story about the greedy man in Luke 12:15-21. How is this man like Al?

8. Woody says at the end that when Andy doesn't want to play with him anymore, "I'll have Buzz Lightyear to keep me company—for infinity and beyond." How long is infinity? Is there anyone you can count on for that long? Read Hebrews 13:5 for the answer.

Follow-Up Activities

Sharing with Others

With your child, gather up toys he or she has outgrown. Talk about how he or she enjoyed them; share fond memories you have about them. Let your child decide which playthings to keep, sell, or give away. Discuss the fact that many kids in the world—including your corner of it—have few toys. Encourage your child to donate used playthings to a local children's hospital or the next Christmas toy drive.

Treasure Hunt

Lend your child a camera (disposable, digital, or other) and challenge him or her to take pictures of the most valuable treasures in your home. Have him or her save one shot for you to use at the end. Use that to take a picture of your family. When you view the pictures, discuss the choices your child made—and how people, who are eternal, are worth far more than cars, jewelry, and electronics.

Just for Fun

Wheezy the Penguin's asthmatic speaking voice is provided by Joe Ranft—one of the movie's writers (and a voice-over artist for *A Bug's Life* and *Finding Nemo*). But when Wheezy's squeaker is fixed at the end of the film and the little guy belts out a big-band version of the song "You've Got a Friend in Me," where does that booming baritone come from? None other than longtime lounge headliner Robert Goulet.

—John Duckworth

Treasure Planet

Rated: PG
Themes: Loyalty, self-sacrifice, the importance of fathers, greed and true wealth, integrity, judging character, honesty, courage, extending mercy, self-confidence, finding your purpose
Running Time: 1 hour, 35 minutes
Starring: The voices of Joseph Gordon-Levitt as Jim Hawkins, Brian Murray as John Silver, David Hyde Pierce as Doctor Doppler, Emma Thompson as Captain Amelia, Martin Short as B.E.N., Michael Wincott as Scroop, Roscoe Lee Browne as Mr. Arrow, Laurie Metcalf as Sarah Hawkins, and Patrick McGoohan as Billy Bones
Based on the novel *Treasure Island* by Robert Louis Stevenson
Directed by: Ron Clements and John Musker

Cautions

This film is rated PG for adventure action and peril, including a couple of treacherous moments, some gunfire, and bloodless swordplay. Yet overall, there's much less swashbuckling here than in Byron Haskin's original 1950s film. Silver's love of the bottle is gone, as are the gruesome battles and general roughness. Still, two characters—one noble, one evil—float off into space, and greedy pirates fall to their doom. Scroop, the villainous spider alien, could creep into the dreams of more impressionable minds. And on the "generally disgusting" meter, a blob alien language sounds like flatulence, and an eyeball bobs to the surface when Silver serves Jim his special soup.

Story Summary

When thrill-seeking, trouble-finding Jim Hawkins is handed the map to the legendary "Treasure Planet," his mother's dog-like scientist friend, Dr. Doppler, decides to fund an expedition. He convinces Jim's mother that he'll watch after him, and once aboard the hired ship, the wind is quickly sucked from their sails as the captain, stern feline Amelia, whittles their excitement down with impressive efficiency. Though distrustful of her rogue crew who are planning mutiny, she assigns young Jim to the Master of the Galley and half-cyborg John Silver.

After quickly bonding with Silver, Jim is blamed for the loss of Mr. Arrow by the underhanded Scroop, who has severed the first mate's lifeline. Silver allows himself to comfort his young friend, but confides to Morph (Polly the parrot's mimicking replacement) that he's "getting in too deep" with Jim, an attachment that puts Silver's lifelong goal of finding Captain Flint's treasure at risk.

After chasing the devious Morph into the galley, Jim overhears Silver denying their friendship to the mutiny-scheming scullery mates. When Silver realizes Jim has overheard the crew's plan, Silver leads the revolt, but Jim, Doppler, and Amelia escape with the map in a space skiff to Treasure Planet. They crash-land and find that meddling Morph has disguised himself as the map. The real map has been left behind on the ship. An abandoned, short-circuited robot,  B.E.N., provides a hideout for the party and leaves with Jim and Morph to retrieve the missing map. Unfortunately, Scroop has stayed behind and very nearly sends Jim to Mr. Arrow's fate. But Jim turns the tide, and Scroop floats off instead.

Meanwhile, Jim returns to find that Silver and crew have captured Amelia and Doppler and are demanding the map. Together, they travel to the mechanical planet's core and locate Flint's treasure—but not without setting off his ancient booby trap. As the spoiled and greedy crewmates descend into the fiery crevasse, Silver is torn between loot and loyalty to his friend. Silver finds his heart and opts to save Jim's life, but now the party must escape the self-destructing planet. Through Jim's bravery and skill, the ship is saved and the celebration is held at Jim's mother's newly-restored restaurant. As Jim's father-figure sails off to other adventures, he assures Jim that he'll always have a friend in him.

Before You Watch

If you've never read Stevenson's original 1883 novel *Treasure Island* together, now may be the time. There are many updated versions as well, so choose what fits your family best. But if you have a young one who is intrigued by pirates and/or ships and sailing, this could be his or her ticket to another world. And having the background for the original story makes the adaptations in *Treasure Planet* that much more interesting.

If your child is interested in space exploration or astronomy, you might also check out some resources on space, stars, and black holes.

Bible Bookmarks

Proverbs 17:13-20; Matthew 19:21; Luke 5:1-11; 1 John 4:7; 2 Corinthians 11:13-14; Matthew 14:27, 10:29-31

Talking Points

1. John Silver is what people call a "sympathetic villain." Even though he is greedy, he is kind and can recognize Jim's potential for greatness. So why do you think John doesn't want to hug Jim? Would you trust John Silver if you were Jim? Read Proverbs 17:13-20 together. What does the Bible say here about friends?

2. According to Proverbs 17:20, do you think John will find what he's seeking? What should he have done after learning that friends are more important than gold? (Read Matthew 19:21 for the answer.)

3. What is it that changes John Silver? (Parents, did love for your children change you? Tell them how.) Read together about love in 1 John 4:7.

4. The role of the totally evil villain is played by the spiderlike alien, Scroop. He's very ugly, but sometimes our enemy isn't so obvious. Read what Paul says about the devil in 2 Corinthians 11:13-14. What

are some ways we can know when something is evil or when it is from God?

5. Have you ever felt like Jim and wanted to seek adventure? What did you do? What kinds of adventures does God offer? Read Luke 5:1-11. What do you suppose Jesus meant by catching men? Do you think it involves adventure? Danger? Risk? Explain.

6. What does Jim's mom say he needs most? Why is that so important? Of all the role models Jim could choose, why do you think he chooses John Silver? Who is the best role model you could choose? (The One who says "follow Me" in Matthew 19:21.) If you were to pick a grown-up to be like, who would that be? Why?

7. What is courage? Do you think you have it? Why or why not? What scares you the most? Some have said courage isn't being fearless, it's doing what's needed even when you're afraid. Who gives courage to face your fears? Read Matthew 14:27.

8. Would you like to have a robotic arm or leg like John Silver? It seems it might be fun at first, but how would you feel if you lost your arm or leg and there weren't any futuristic replacements for you? Do you know anyone who doesn't have a certain part or is different in some way? How do you think they feel when they can't do things others can? What did Jesus think of people who are different? Read Matthew 10:29-31.

Follow-Up Activities

"Recycled Life" Stories

Like the movie *Treasure Planet,* God is into recycling old, familiar lives and making them new. If you've never shared your testimony, take this opportunity to share about your conversion to Christianity. In what ways did God take your old life and make it new? If you feel inclined, make it a special ceremony in which each of you who has experienced a "recycled life" shares some of the new ways of thinking and living you've noticed in yourself since becoming a Christian.

Treasure Hunt

Everyone will need a Bible for this game. The object is to find the stories (as indicated by the clues provided) as quickly as possible—before time runs out or anyone else can find them. The family member who finds the most the fastest wins the prize. (The prize could be anything valuable to your child: candy, a special privilege, etc.) Use a stopwatch, and depending on participants' Bible knowledge and ages, allow 30 seconds to one minute for each clue. (A parent can help younger kids, or the family can play as two teams.) Some of the clues yield one answer, others will have multiple possibilities. Answers are given below.

The Clues
1. A "rule of gold"
2. A huge seafaring vessel
3. A talking beast
4. An innocent man who lost enormous wealth
5. The close friendship of a future king
6. Three men escape from a furnace
7. A boy's display of courage against a giant enemy
8. Paul's "true son in the faith"

The Answers
1. *The Golden Rule: Matthew 7:12*
2. *Noah's Ark: Genesis 6*
3. *Balaam's Donkey: Numbers 22:28*
4. *Job: Job 1*
5. *David and Jonathan: 1 Samuel 18*
6. *Shadrach, Meshach, and Abednego: Daniel 3*
7. *David and Goliath: 1 Samuel 17*
8. *Timothy: 1 Timothy 1:2*

Just for Fun

The animation supervisor for John Silver was the veteran animator Glen Keane, son of Bil Keane, the cartoonist of *Family Circus*.

In his dad's comics, Glen was the inspiration for Billy, the cute little towheaded brother with all the funny sayings, scurrying around the yard and getting into things. Now he scurries around animating feature films and gets into pencils and paints.

—*Mick Silva*

The Wizard of Oz

Rated: G
Themes: Value of home, love and family, compassion, courage, hopes and dreams, finding your purpose, good vs. evil, contentment, self-worth
Running Time: 1 hour, 52 minutes
Starring: Judy Garland as Dorothy, Frank Morgan as the Wizard, Ray Bolger as Scarecrow, Bert Lahr as Cowardly Lion, Jack Haley as Tin Man, Margaret Hamilton as the Wicked Witch of the West, Billie Burke as Glinda, Charley Grapewin as Uncle Henry, and Clara Blandick as Auntie Em
Based on the book by L. Frank Baum
Directed by: Victor Fleming (among others)

 ## Cautions

The Wizard of Oz has been scaring young children since 1939. Even without the bloody elements that typify most classic fairy tales, the scariness level of this film can be high depending on the particular sensitivity level of the child. Most adults will remember being terrified of one part or another—menacing scenes with the evil witch, the flying monkeys, or the disembodied wizard head. Please use caution with young children and warn them beforehand of what could be the more frightening aspects for them.

Other than that, Uncle Henry is a passive-aggressive male role model, and Auntie Em implies plenty when she tells Miss Gulch that "being a Christian woman," she can't say what she really thinks of her.

Story Summary

One of 15 films categorized as "art" on the Vatican film list and the "greatest family film of all time" (American Film Institute), *The Wizard of Oz* stands as one of the most enduring and definitive film experiences in American history. L. Frank Baum wrote "the classic American fairy tale" in 1900 about a young heroine, Dorothy Gale, dreaming of fairylands and fearing the realities of everyday life on a Kansas farm.

When little dog Toto narrowly escapes destruction by crusty Elmira Gulch, Dorothy is determined to run away. On the road, a kindly fortuneteller plays a goodhearted trick to make Dorothy remember her Auntie Em's love and concern, and she and Toto race home as a tornado whirls on the horizon. While her family takes cover in the storm cellar, Dorothy is left in the house and winds up unconscious after a blow to the head. When she comes to, the house is twirling inside the twister, as evidenced by various creatures— including Elmira Gulch on her bicycle—floating by the window. When Elmira suddenly  transforms into a witch on a broomstick, clearly this is not your everyday Kansas tornado.

The farmhouse lands with a jolt and as Dorothy and Toto rise, they open the front door onto a Technicolor Munchkinland. Glinda, the Good Witch, arrives to point out that the house has landed on the Wicked Witch of the East, and Dorothy is now the rightful owner of the coveted ruby slippers. Inevitably, the Wicked Witch of the West (Elmira Gulch, transformed) visits to promise destruction. But a well-placed threat sends her packing and Glinda points Dorothy to the yellow brick road, which leads to the Emerald City and the Wizard, who will tell her how she can return home.

Along her way, Dorothy is joined by a talking Scarecrow, a rusty Tin Man, and a Cowardly Lion, each in search of a missing essential element they hope the Wizard will bestow.

Through turns perilous and precipitous, they reach the Emerald City, but not before the Wicked Witch casts a sleep spell. Resourceful Glinda sends snow to rouse them, and they enter the city to meet the great and powerful Oz. But before he grants their requests he requires a fee: the Wicked Witch's broomstick. Dejected but resolute, the crew sets out for the Witch's castle only to be assaulted by her flying monkeys, who carry off Dorothy and Toto.

The determined friends pursue Dorothy and Toto and enter the castle disguised as guards. They free the captives, but the Witch is waiting with her army. Just as it appears all is lost, Dorothy unwittingly melts the Witch with a bucket of water, and the stunned but grateful guards hand over the broomstick.

The band returns victorious to the Wizard and present his required sacrifice. But he is noncompliant—that is, until Toto reveals him as the "man behind the curtain." Revealed, the Wizard accepts Dorothy's scolding and delivers each hopeful with the quality most desired. As for Dorothy, she is offered a ride back to Kansas when the Wizard makes his exit in a hot air balloon.

The day arrives, but Toto spies a cat in the crowd, and forced to chase afer him, Dorothy misses her ride. She's ready to give up when Glinda arrives to save the day with news that the ruby slippers were Dorothy's ticket home all along. Dorothy clicks her heels and wakes up in Kansas, surrounded by her family and filled with the wisdom that "there's no place like home."

Before You Watch

Explain that in this story there are good witches and bad witches, but in real life, there are no good witches. Anyone who calls himself or herself a witch today is far different from the witches in this movie. Pictures of wicked witches who ride broomsticks on Halloween are make-believe, but witches in today's society are real people who need Jesus. (See Deuteronomy 18:10 and Galatians 5:19-21 for a biblical view of witchcraft.)

Bible Bookmarks
Psalm 27; Revelation 21:10-27; Luke 15:11-24

Talking Points

1. The Scarecrow believes himself to be brainless, yet he is in fact the most clever of Dorothy's companions. When we talk about "smarts," what does it mean? Do you think you are smart, or do you feel more often like the Scarecrow, wishing you were smarter? Read 1 Corinthians 8:1-3. What does Paul value more than being smart?

2. Many people's favorite character is the Cowardly Lion. When he resolves to rescue Dorothy from the Wicked Witch's castle, the Lion proves he's capable of great courage, yet he still believes he's a coward. Why do you suppose this is? (He thinks courage is being without fear, rather than acting even when he's afraid.) Read about the greatest source of courage in Psalm 27.

3. The Tin Man is also far from being heartless; he's the most sensitive character in the story. Each of the three friends already possess what he seeks. Is this true in life? What we believe about ourselves often determines who we are. The journey to the Emerald City requires the characters to believe in themselves and make the most of their gifts to get there. Is there a trait you feel you lack that you might actually already have?

4. What is the purpose of Dorothy's journey? What do you think she learned? If you imagine yourself on a journey in life right now, what is your Emerald City? Do you want to do well in school, maybe get accepted to a club or team? Dorothy's biggest ally is Glinda the Good Witch of the North. Though God is your ultimate help, who is another Glinda in your life who can help you reach your goal?

5. What's the difference between pretending and lying? When the Wizard is pretending to be the great and powerful Oz, is he lying? Why do you suppose some people say someone is "telling a story" when they mean "telling lies"? Are stories the same as lies? Why or why not?

6. In this movie, there is the classic fight between the good guys and the bad guys which the good guys ultimately win. How did you feel when the Wicked Witch melts? Did you expect something else to happen? Why do you suppose we enjoy seeing the bad guys lose?

Follow-Up Activities
Prodigal Son

Some people have related this story to the parable of the prodigal son in Luke 15:11-24. Have a parent read that passage while two volunteers act out the parts of the father and the son as it's read. If you have enough family members, you can add the brother and some servants. Make it more fun by dressing up in robes or sheets. Let everyone take a turn acting out the parts. After the story's been read once, the actors might want to ad-lib their parts, including some likely dialogue and actions. Conclude the game with a "prodigal son" feast featuring a special dinner and dessert.

"Who's Your Friend?" Game
Take turns blindfolding and leading each other through the "forest"—one or more rooms in your house. Have one family member give friendly commands (ones that help the child reach the goal) and another give unfriendly commands (ones that confuse or lead the child astray). Instruct the sojourner to listen carefully to the friendly commands and ignore the unfriendly ones. Once he or she makes it through the forest, talk about how it became clear who was the friendly person to listen to and who was the enemy. Discuss how in life it becomes clear who is a friend and who is not by the advice they give. Who in the movie was not a good person to listen to?

Just for Fun

When the movie was made in 1939, Shirley Temple was originally considered for the role of Dorothy. (If your kids have never seen a Shirley Temple movie, consider renting one sometime.) Ultimately, it was decided that Judy Garland would be the best person for the role of Dorothy since she was older than Shirley and had such an excellent singing voice.

—*Mick Silva*

About the Writers

Brandy Bruce holds a Bachelor of Arts degree in English from Liberty University, where she currently works in the College of General Studies. She resides in Lynchburg, Virginia, with her husband, Jeff, and their cat, Georgia.

Jan P. Dennis is the president of The Jan P. Dennis Literary Agency. With over 25 years of publishing experience, he has worked with Stephen R. Lawhead, Frank Peretti, T. Davis Bunn, Francis Schaeffer, Charles Colson, Max Lucado, Bodie Thoene, Ravi Zacharias, and many other prominent authors. Most recently he has helped establish the career of Ted Dekker.

John Duckworth is a senior book producer at Focus on the Family. The author of several books, he is also the father of twin boys who watch entirely too many motion pictures.

John Fornof writes and directs for *Adventures in Odyssey*, a family radio drama heard on over 700 stations. He's producer for the new *Last Chance Detectives* radio series. John was also the writer, voice director, and associate producer for *Ribbits!*—an award-winning computer-animated program produced by Focus on the Family.

Lissa Halls Johnson is a book producer, writer, and fiction acquisitions editor for Focus on the Family. She is the creator and editor of the "Brio Girls" book series. She has written 16 novels for teenagers and young readers.

Tom Neven is a graduate of Wheaton College and Columbia University. He was editor of *Focus on the Family* magazine for six years and is currently a senior editor for *Plugged In* magazine. He has written and edited for several book publishers and is also a contributing columnist to the *Denver Post*.

Mick Silva graduated from Westmont College in 1996 and married his junior high sweetheart in 2000. As a new dad, he is also a highly-distracted associate editor in Focus on the Family's book publishing department.

Larry Weeden is the director of book development for Focus on the Family and has written or co-authored 20 books.

FOCUS ON THE FAMILY®

Welcome to the Family!

Whether you received this book as a gift, borrowed it, or purchased
it yourself, we're glad you read it. It's just one of the many helpful,
insightful, and encouraging resources produced by Focus on the Family.

In fact, that's what Focus on the Family is
all about—providing inspiration, information, and
biblically based advice to people in all stages of life.

It began in 1977 with the vision of one man, Dr. James Dobson,
a licensed psychologist and author of 18 best-selling books on marriage,
parenting, and family. Alarmed by the societal, political, and
economic pressures that were threatening the existence of the American
family, Dr. Dobson founded Focus on the Family with one employee
and a once-a-week radio broadcast aired on only 36 stations.

Now an international organization, the ministry is dedicated to
preserving Judeo-Christian values and strengthening and encouraging
families through the life-changing message of Jesus Christ.
Focus ministries reach families worldwide through 10 separate
radio broadcasts, two television news features, 13 publications,
18 Web sites, and a steady series of books and award-winning
films and videos for people of all ages and interests.

• • •

For more information about the ministry, or if we can be of help to your
family, simply write to Focus on the Family, Colorado Springs, CO 80995
or call (800) A-FAMILY (232-6459). Friends in Canada may write
Focus on the Family, PO Box 9800, Stn Terminal, Vancouver, BC V6B 4G3 or
call (800) 661-9800. Visit our Web site—www.family.org—to learn more about
Focus on the Family or to find out if there is an associate office in your country.

We'd love to hear from you!

The Next Video You Rent Could Change Your Teen's Life

Movie Nights

Teach your teens to be discerning when they choose a movie. *Movie Nights* converts 25 entertaining, thought-provoking films, like *The Princess Bride, Apollo 13* and *Groundhog Day,* to name a few, into dynamic opportunities to connect with your teens and help them critically evaluate the media they consume. Each "Movie Night" presents a practical process for watching each movie, featuring discussion questions, activities, related Scriptures and more to spark discussion. Your teens learn to develop critical thinking to evaluate movies from a biblical worldview. Paperback.

"This book offers a valuable concept, skillfully executed. *Movie Nights* is an important faith-based attempt to use the best in our popular culture to elevate as well as entertain, and to encourage dedication along with diversion."
—Michael Medved, *film critic, nationally syndicated radio host*

• • •

What Greater Gift Can You Give Your Children Than One That Lasts For Eternity?

Parents' Guide to the Spiritual Growth of Children

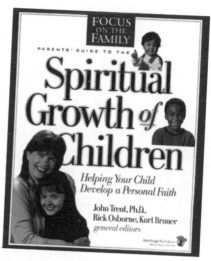

Passing on a foundation of faith to your child is an awesome responsibility. Now, the job is easier with Heritage Builders' *Parents' Guide to the Spiritual Growth of Children,* co-authored by best-selling author John Trent and Rick Osborne. Simple, practical and comprehensive, it's a terrific tool for developing your child's Christian values from birth to age 12. Filled with answers to the questions parents have most, it's a reassuring guide that helps you make sure your child is progressing spiritually. No matter where you are in your Christian walk, this guide will encourage you that passing on a strong spiritual heritage is possible. Available in hardcover and paperback.

"I can't think of a more important task for parents than passing their Christian faith to their children. Heritage Builders gives parents easy-to-use plans and ideas to help them pass their faith; this couldn't come at a better time for our children and culture."
—Gary Smalley, *Author, speaker and founder of Smalley Relationship Center*

• • •

Look for these special books in your Christian bookstore or request a copy by calling (800) A-FAMILY (232-6459). Friends in Canada may write Focus on the Family, PO Box 9800, Stn Terminal, Vancouver, BC V6B 4G3 or call (800) 661-9800.

Visit our Web site (www.family.org) to learn more about the ministry or find out if there is a Focus on the Family office in your country.

Spark Spiritual Growth:
Make A Date For Family Nights

Family Nights Tool Chest

How do you get kids to stop playing long enough to learn something important? You don't! You combine fun and spiritual growth in a memory-making time called Family Night. *An Introduction to Family Nights Tool Chest* shows you how to pass on Christian values using an ordinary object like toothpaste. And when you make learning a game, kids 12 and under have no trouble understanding the importance of being obedient, resisting temptation, and more! Paperback.

Jim Weidmann is one of the founders of Heritage Builders and developed the Family Nights concept several years ago. He also serves as vice chairman of National Day of Prayer and executive director of Heritage Builders. Jim and his wife have four children.

Kurt Bruner is co-author with J. Otis Ledbetter of *Your Heritage*. He has spent nearly 20 years with Focus on the Family where he currently serves as group vice president of Media and Communications Support. He and his wife have four children.

•   •   •

Look for these special books in your Christian bookstore or request a
copy by calling (800) A-FAMILY (232-6459). Friends in Canada
may write Focus on the Family, PO Box 9800, Stn Terminal,
Vancouver, BC V6B 4G3 or call (800) 661-9800.

Visit our Web site (www.family.org) to learn more about the ministry
or find out if there is a Focus on the Family office in your country.